Pr

Here Comes the Moo

" … a book of great charm."
—Bettyjane Wylie, CM, award winning author

"It's a delight! Both the prose pieces and the poems are so accessible and quietly wise. I like too the quirky illustrations."
—Lesley Duncan, *The Herald*, UK

Shanghai Scarlet

"A remarkably mature and articulate homage to 1930s Shanghai. … A superb novel. … Both (Shanghai) books are classics."
—Katherine Byrnell, reader, Canada

"(An) impressive historical novel. … This is a sensitive, thoughtful and poignant story. The ending is very effective."
—Professor Poshek Fu, University of Illinois, Urbana – Champaign

"The world of 1930s Shanghai is vividly brought to life in Margaret Blair's *Shanghai Scarlet*. … it winds its way through the wonderfully portrayed intellectual and social world of a city on the brink of major upheaval."
—Historical Novel Society

Gudao Lone Islet, The War Years in Shanghai, a childhood memoir

"Thank you for having written such an excellent book. I would very much like to quote extracts of your book in mine. It is beautifully written, very vivid and tragic and uplifting by turns."
—Nicola Tyrer, author, *Stolen Childhoods, The Untold Story of the Children Interned by the Japanese in the Second World War* UK

"Congratulations on the fascinating, wonderful book."
—Professor John Meehan S. J., Campion College, Canada

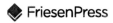

Suite 300 - 990 Fort St
Victoria, BC, V8V 3K2
Canada

www.friesenpress.com

Copyright © 2017 by Margaret Blair
First Edition — 2017

All rights reserved.

www.margaretblair.com

Cover designs and Map by Margaret Blair and Gary Moon

Certain stock imagery by Thinkstock

Photographs: Toys on chair (Margaret Blair), Harriston Public Library, Reading Mouse and some cover photography (Gary Moon)

Others from Wikipedia and www.thinkstockphotos.com

No part of this publication may be reproduced in any form, or by any means, electronic or mechanical, including photocopying, recording, or any information browsing, storage, or retrieval system, without permission in writing from FriesenPress.

ISBN
978-1-4602-9863-3 (Hardcover)
978-1-4602-9864-0 (Paperback)
978-1-4602-9865-7 (eBook)

1. HISTORY, CANADA

Distributed to the trade by The Ingram Book Company

For Nicholas, Ariane and David

Table of Contents

Preface • viii

Map of Central Canada, Southern Ontario • ix

THE NATURAL WORLD
Family Reunion • 3
Rainbows • 5
Spring Song • 7
Monologue of a Cat on her Fate • 9
Here Comes the Moon ... • 11
The Sixth Line and Beehive Lane • 13
Raccoons and Christopher Columbus • 17
How Much Wood Would a Woodchuck Chuck? • 21
The Maitland Valley Conservation Authority • 23
Country Adventure • 25

MAKING A DIFFERENCE
Author's Note (William of Malmesbury) • 29
Scene with Cat in Malmesbury Abbey • 31
Poem to William of Malmesbury • 34
Joyfully Towards Eighty-one We Go! • 35
Proton Township Farmer's Daughter – Agnes Macphail • 37
Carnegie Libraries • 43
Nellie McClung • 47
Chad Martin of Palmerston – How One Thing Led to Another • 51
John McCrae – poet, artist, soldier and doctor • 55

DAILY LIFE
Spring, That Joyful Season • 63
Books • 65
The National Historic Site that Almost Never Was • 67
Elora Writers' Festival • 69
Let's Tanka • 73
Funeral • 73
Biological Clock • 74
Beginnings – To an Eighteen-Year-Old • 75
Stop, We're Canadian • 77
Have You Ever Wondered? • 79
South Sea Islands and Fire-breathing Dragons • 81
Thanksgiving • 83
Remembrance • 85
Raggedy Ann, Golliwog and Little Black Sambo • 89
Christmas Reading • 93
A Poem for the Season • 95
Christmas Cozy • 95
Carols on the Sixth Line • 97

The Author • 101

Suggested Discussion Guide for Book Clubs • 103

Preface

For reading and discussing the collected pieces, I would like to thank Jennifer Glossop, Helen Thompson and Bettyjane Wylie. Their comments have enhanced the writing. I also thank Dorothy McLelland for her discussion about the number of essays to include in a book of this type. As always, the book has benefitted from Gary Moon's execution of the front and back cover designs, map and illustrations, including photography of the reading mouse which is on the title page, inner section pages and after the last page of text. Sincere thanks go to the Ink and Cookies Writing Group. Without them this book would not exist. Ably led now by Trudy MacMillan, the diverse group of people who love to write has been meeting for 30 years. Current writers are the following: Betty Audet, Doris and Tom Cassan, Linda Dunk, Anne Grobbo, Jean Kuehn, Grace and Royden McCoag, Janet Murphy and Marian Pinnell.

A local magazine, *The Rural Route*, asked my writing group to contribute. I decided to meet this challenge, and judging from the positive feedback on what I wrote, it seems reasonable to share these contributions, and ten other pieces, with a broader readership.

Margaret Blair,
Minto, 2017

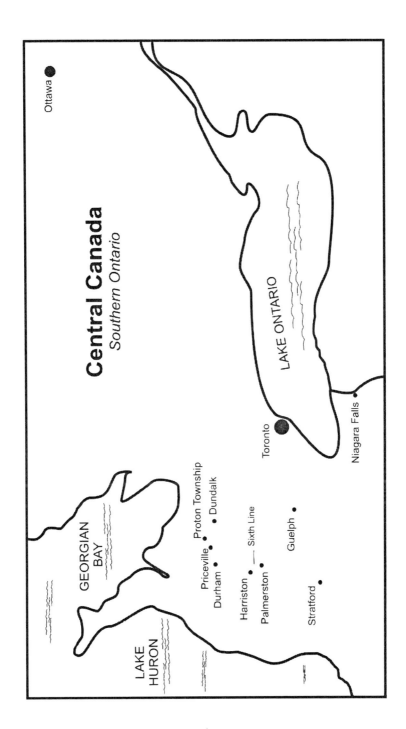

THE NATURAL WORLD

HERE COMES THE MOON

Family Reunion

Fall ushers in a time for family reunions at Thanksgiving, Christmas and New Year, and what would they be without food? This story is different from the others about these reunions: it took place in Spring, but is also accompanied by that essential ingredient.

I was weeding the raised flowerbed by our door, when out from under the deck beside it popped a tiny bandit face, about three inches across. Almost immediately, it was surrounded by four more little faces, each blinking at the light. I thought, *Baby raccoons deserve to enjoy the sun as much as I do.* So off I went to do some work in another part of the garden, leaving them in peace. When I later mentioned the event to Ronald, my husband, he huffed a bit, saying he understood raccoons could damage the house foundations. However, since we had heard no digging noises, we assumed the mother was simply using the space under our deck as a den to bring up her young.

The next afternoon I returned to my flowerbed, when out popped the five tiny raccoons again. They settled themselves in a heap to nap, just like kittens, and once more I left them to enjoy the sun. When I returned, the babies had all gone, except for one. It lay dead among the flowers. Ronald took a shovel and disposed of the small remains by the river that runs round our garden.

We had never before seen such young animals out by themselves and decided they must be in some trouble. Ronald speculated that the mother had been caught in a trap or shot, and that the babies were out looking for her. We were wondering what if anything we could do next, when the four little raccoons came out yet again to the flowerbed.

"Maybe I should call the OSPCA," I said, and was turning to find their number when Ronald, who was still looking out of the window, said, "Wait. Come and see this."

Limping through the trees and across the grass came the mother raccoon, holding before her one mangled, bleeding foreleg. That leg seemed shorter than the other, and I wondered whether the paw was missing altogether, left behind in the trap. (I had read that sometimes animals chew themselves free, losing a limb.) Somehow, the raccoon dragged herself up onto the flowerbed. Then after much joyful nuzzling and tender raccoon-speak, she shepherded her remaining brood back into their den to be fed.

We had witnessed a bittersweet family reunion.

Rainbows

Early in a recent year, many living around the Seven Bridges Road, which runs off our own Sixth Line, saw a very rare sight in the sky. No, it wasn't a UFO, it was a perfect twinned rainbow: we could see both ends of it, with the colours continuing uninterrupted across the whole semicircle of the arc. Two rain showers, with different sized droplets, had combined to form the bow.

Although a number saw this unusual light phenomenon, no one could have been so lucky as to find the fabled pot of gold at either end, for scientific reasons; a viewer can see the rainbow only at a 42 degree angle. As one walks towards it, the bow recedes, always keeping the distance needed for the 42 degree angle.

For centuries, scientists have been studying the rainbow. Their written conclusions go back as far as Aristotle in fourth century BC Greece. He concluded that the rainbow is caused by reflected light, and that the colours are not permanent, as in painted objects. Later, in the eleventh century AD, scientists in Persia and China agreed with this conclusion, with the further insight from the Chinese that the rainbow is the result of sunlight meeting droplets of rain in the air, an observation that agrees with modern studies.

Rainbows continued to engage scientists such as Roger Bacon, René Descartes and, in the late seventeenth to eighteenth centuries, Isaac Newton, who cracked the rainbow code. Using a glass prism, he defined the rainbow's colours as red, orange, yellow, green, blue, indigo and violet, each colour refracting at a different angle. Many associate these seven colours with the seven notes of a musical scale. Those people with synaesthesia not only hear music as it is played, but also see it as the colours of the rainbow. (On a sunny day, it is possible to see the rainbow and its colours near waterfalls and fountains – even garden sprinklers. Niagara Falls is a fine place for rainbow enthusiasts.)

HERE COMES THE MOON

No doubt since the beginning of our time as humans when we began to think about the world around us, we have been creating myths about the rainbow's meaning. In Genesis, God gives the rainbow to Noah as a token of his covenant with the earth's creatures that he will not again destroy them by flood. Among ancient people, a common perception of the rainbow is as a bridge between heaven and earth, between gods and mortals.

On a philosophical note, the span of a rainbow is made up of both rain and sunshine, just like the span of a normal life. In the present day Western world, the rainbow has become a symbol of hope for those suffering illness or sorrow. The poet William Wordsworth said it well when he wrote "My heart leaps up when I behold a rainbow in the sky."

Spring Song

Robin's tune
Green-blue eggs in nest
Blue-white sky
Forget-me-not drifts
Dandelions
Violets in grass
Groundhog's blink
Half blind and woolly
Happy jump
Of rabbits eating
New green growth
Apple tree in bloom
Tea in hand
On the deck feet bare
Country Spring
All that is joyful

Monologue of a Cat on her Fate

(a cat abandoned on a farm road)

There are cats – and cats. I did not come with papers from the breeder to sit on a special chair and be played with and fed delicious morsels in my own bowl with my name on it, to drink from a fountain of fresh water and to be respectfully, gently groomed. *I* was disposable. *I* could be thrown away.

At first I lay in a cardboard box with my soft warm mother. Children played with and petted me. Then came the ride in a car and the toss out onto a gritty road by a creek. For a long time I wandered by the stream, drinking the water and finding no food, until I stumbled across a field into a large space with enormous animals and other cats. I caught a mouse, and lived. I made a friend: the large cat, black like me.

The large black found the house across the big field, where we had food several times a day and water in a bowl. In good weather, we lay in the sun and didn't have to fight, and we weren't afraid. At night we returned to the large place.

Then a machine, at the place where we slept, caught my front leg. I managed to pull it out and dragged myself to the house across the big field, and slept in their small shed for a while. The people still fed us (the large black and me), and while my leg was painful, one of our meals each day was a wonderful one of special food they called salmon, mixed with something they called bread. After that food I would lie on a bed of dry leaves on top of the lavender, and sleep and sleep. That's when I began to heal. One person there helped me clean myself until my leg again had fur on it. But my paw never returned to its earlier condition. Now I could clean all of me by myself; the dot of white fur at the end of my tail really shone in the sun. But from then on I limped.

HERE COMES THE MOON

We continued our better life, the large black and me. Sometimes, the kind person would sit beside us and stroke my back. I felt happy. It reminded me of when I was with my mother in that other house. As the growing things in the field by "our" house grew tall, we caught mice there. They too were looking for food. When the snow came, we used to go to our house by walking along the road and up the path. A huge machine always cleared the snow from them.

But then came more machines at the large place where I slept. They dug up a huge mound of earth and me with it for, you see, I am deaf and could not hear the shovel coming. I died after a long time in pain. I couldn't breathe under the soil.

The people across the big field will never know what happened to me, the cat that was disposable, the cat that could be thrown away.

Here Comes the Moon …

… the harvest moon, that is. We have all had the experience of driving east on a local road to be confronted by the wonderfully large and yellow harvest moon just coming up. It seems about to crash into the earth and roll along the road towards us, flattening the car. An hour or two later, it is floating serenely high in the sky, making us think, *Whew! That was a close one – but we're safe for another year.*

To spoil the magic, here comes the explanation for the phenomenon: the harvest moon is the full moon closest to the autumn equinox. A shorter than usual rising time between successive moon rises around this season means that the plane of the moon's orbit round the earth makes a narrow angle with respect to the horizon in the evening. This low-hanging moon appears larger and more colourful than usual.

In olden days, humans regarded the full moon with superstitious dread: the cause of madness and werewolves. Across a background of the full moon, witches rode their broomsticks and wolves howled. Nowadays, we know that the moon really does affect many aspects of our life here on earth, such as the tides of the oceans. A man has walked on the moon and jumped high in his heavy clothing, giving us a practical demonstration of the moon's gravity, which is about one-fifth that of the earth's. More recently scientists, watching the arc of large bodies from space most likely to hit the earth, have used the moon as a marker. They track only those passing between the moon's orbit and the earth.

But enough of the facts … so much has been written, and songs sung, about this mysterious satellite of the earth. Its name happens to rhyme with June, the month of weddings and honeymoons (there's that word again). Couples linger romantically by the light of this, our planet's only satellite. Some people reading this now will remember the old song that says: "The moon belongs to everyone. The best things in life are free." My favourite quotation comes from the inimitable Walter de la Mare. It is from his poem "Silver" which begins:

HERE COMES THE MOON

"Slowly, silently, now the moon
Walks the night in her silver shoon;
This way, and that, she peers and sees
Silver fruit upon silver trees."

The first time I became aware of the moon – I mean *really* noticed it – was at the age of five, on a holiday to Japan. There, we visited a local family with a house some way along the beach from ours. It was constructed of the traditional Japanese light removable panels of wood with paper.

"Then Ah Ling takes me to visit a Japanese family whose house also overlooks the beach. The Japanese greet us ceremoniously with many bows. They pass tea and different kinds of little cakes, fruit and sweets from person to person. The adults don't ignore me but treat me with great kindness and respect. I think I am the lucky one. It is a wonderful way to end the day.
When the sun is setting the men remove one side of the room overlooking the sea and we enjoy the glorious sunset. As we talk quietly, the bright colours of the evening sky gradually darken to blend in with the sea. This is a holy time. The family calls it their sunset-viewing room.
Then we move to another room where we lounge on futons and eat more little cakes with tea. This time the men have removed part of the ceiling and I gaze up at the black velvet sky with its millions of stars. We never see this in the city, but with no lights on outside, the stars shine out quite clearly. They seem so near that I could stretch out my hand and pick a few.
After a while we all lie with our heads on hard rolled pillows. There is a kind of ringing silence. I wonder whether we're supposed to go to sleep, and sneak a look at the others. But no, they're still looking at the sky. I look back up. And then it happens: sailing slowly across our window in the ceiling comes the large yellow lantern of the moon.
There is a collective, soft 'Ahhh ...'"

The Sixth Line and Beehive Lane

The Rural Route has had wonderful contributions from our neighbours Ruth Anne and Howard Savage, describing life on the part of Sixth Line where we live. It is a magical land of rural residential and farm properties, and bush. There, various types of wildlife continue to have their habitat near enough to be seen close up by those of us lucky enough to live there.

Frogs, garter snakes and toads live along the several tributaries of the Maitland River that cross our Line. Cottontail rabbits, raccoons and woolly, half blind groundhogs graze on the mix of greenery growing in the summer months. Spring would not be spring without the rabbits jumping for joy after every few bites as they taste the new growth.

Even the fluffy grey opossum, the only marsupial in North America (it keeps its young ones, born fully developed, in a pouch until they're bigger), has found a home here. The opossum originated in South America, but with global warming has been making its way north.

Foxes tend to keep to the night, but on one daylight occasion, a fox chased our cat up a tree. It soon took off when we went out to see what the cat's cries were about. Another encounter we had with a nocturnal animal occurred when we were coming along a side road after midnight and saw a huge porcupine slowly making its way along the road in front of the car. We duly slowed down and fell in line behind. After a few yards, the porcupine veered off the road to let us pass, turned round and gave us a really grumpy look. "Why are you day folk invading my space?" it seemed to say.

Birds return in February, with black-capped chickadees and red cardinals in the vanguard, their vivid colouring flashing out against the snow. The ready supply of food, water and trees in the Sixth Line provides perfect conditions for nesting. The birds' busyness flying around, making nests, feeding their young and calling at sunrise adds

HERE COMES THE MOON

new life to the place. At the farm across the road, the rooster joins in, telling everyone when the sun comes up and also when it's going down.

Despite the many other more suitable places, some birds still insist on invading the little balcony outside our bedroom. For several years, one pair nested in our mailbox and we had to pay for one in town until September.

In the first week of August most of the birds leave. Then the Sixth Line provides a resting place for migrating flocks. They usually stay for about 20 minutes and chatter loudly in the trees and on the telephone wire; sometimes they are so exhausted they just sit, in rather eerie silence. In late autumn, great blue heron stop to eat fish from the Maitland creeks beside our garden and across the road.

Initially, Sixth Line families were farmers and had names reminiscent of the British Isles. They always had a strong community spirit. This farming aspect has continued, though now a few retirees (mostly farm) and others live there. As more immigrants came, the names took on a wider European flavour and in more recent years, the Line has welcomed a substantial contingent of Mennonites. For over 30 years, carol singers have gone along the Line on Christmas Eve, joined lately by Mennonites who continue the strong community spirit the Line has always presented.

As they became more prosperous, residents built schools. Initially, these had one room with all grades taught by one teacher. In the late 1800s, Glenlee School was built at the corner of Lot 5, and at one time it catered to two families only, each sending ten children. Lately, the school has been substantially renovated into a private home, still with the old school bell. However across the road another school, with two rooms and two teachers, has been built for the Mennonite children. There they play skipping and hide-and-go-seek near the school building, and enjoy baseball games and skating on a rink in winter in the field beyond. They, too, have a year's end concert for parents. So the Sixth Line continues to change but remain the same.

Pictures of the school children printed in *Minto Memories* show poignantly the progress over time. Children in the 1920s and early 1930s look serious, even sad, and are not well clothed (some photographed with no shoes). One imagines the hard work they put in on chores after five in the morning before setting off for school. Later school photos for the area show a more cheerful and prosperous crowd.

THE NATURAL WORLD

In *Minto Memories,* a school photo of Glenlee 1906 – 1908 shows Alice, Donald and Archie McTaggart, who lived on our Part Lot 10. Archie left his mark. His name is still visible, carved into the door of an old miniature barn behind our garage. His brother thought this was a good idea and decided to put his name below Archie's. Poor Donald chose a noisier way of doing it: making the name in dots from a nail hammered in. He had hardly started when a parent must have come out to see what was causing the racket – and confiscated the hammer. The name was never finished. Donald died quite young, but his brother Archie became a teacher in Toronto. Sister Alice lived at home to care for her mother and ended her days in Harriston.

There are many tales to tell of the east Sixth Line, which meanders down to cross Highway 9 (running south out of Harriston) and becomes a dead end called Beehive Lane. What is now a picnic area on the corner was once a one-room school called SS #1 Beehive. Within living memory (1953) Beehive School was invaded for a whole week by bees taking their rightful place. But that's another story …

HERE COMES THE MOON

Raccoons and Christopher Columbus

We are all aware of raccoons, those cute nocturnal rascals we see around (especially in springtime) that we love to hate. I've found out a number of things I didn't know about them, including how to keep them at a distance if required.

Raccoons are omnivorous, ideally eating one-third of their meals from each of the following categories: plants, insects and grubs, and fish. Although they have few predators, raccoons die mainly through encounters with cars, their top running speed being only 15 miles per hour. In the wild, these animals live up to only three years. Raccoons in captivity live much longer: up to 20 years. Some hundreds of years ago, they were kept as pets in South America, and famously by Calvin Coolidge, American president from 1923 to 1929 and his wife Grace, who named their raccoon pet, Rebecca.

Physically, the raccoons' longer hind legs give them a hump-backed appearance when on the move. These animals can rotate their hind feet 180 degrees, allowing them to climb down trees head first. Breeding season starts in February, and after two months, up to five or six kits appear. Raccoons fatten up during summer, and although they don't actually hibernate, they stay inside their dens most of winter, during which time they can go without food. About 90 percent of the raccoon's fur is under-fur to keep them warm.

In rural areas, raccoons tend to have as many as 20 places they use for living space, sometimes for only a day. Every so often we have a female raccoon bringing up kits under our deck for a month or two before moving on. The kits stay with their mother for over a year. With their bandit faces, raccoons are very cute but as with all wild animals, should be left strictly alone. Occasionally, raccoons can carry diseases such as rabies and roundworm.

HERE COMES THE MOON

We tend to think of these animals as living in parts of the Americas only, but they have been successfully introduced to other countries, and now roam Germany, Russia and the islands of Japan. Christopher Columbus was the first European to inform others about the raccoon, which he thought was a kind of dog kept by some Caribbean people as a pet. He took several back to Europe and exhibited them in Portugal where they soon died. On his return to North America, Columbus fed sailors on raccoon meat to the point that the animal became extinct on the island where he made his headquarters. Raccoons have continued to be food for poorer people in the Southern United States of America.

In the 1600s, Captain John Smith (famously linked with the First Nations princess Pocohontas) mentioned these animals, by which time their name was more like the modern one. In Powhatan, the language of Algonquins, they were named *arakunen*, meaning "he who scratches with his hands." By the seventeenth century, raccoon pelts were traded (though Davy Crockett probably did not wear the hat as portrayed by Fess Parker in the Disney film). Low-ranking officials of Tennessee were paid in raccoon pelts. Later a coat made from them was fashionable in the Roaring Twenties, especially for men.

Raccoons are insatiably curious. They pick up anything they can find, examine then drop it. We learned the hard way not to leave statues on plinths or large china flowerpots in the little open barn at the back. They even stole a plate and kept it under the deck for three years before it turned up again. Objects you don't want broken should be locked in the garage – or like our big, wise old stone owl, should be too heavy for a raccoon to move.

At a city house, we once rolled out strips of sod on a bare patch of lawn. For some time, our neighbours were treated over breakfast to the amusing sight of us rushing out to fold down the strips, which had been neatly rolled up during the night by raccoons looking for grubs. The grass never grew. The next year, a more thoughtful neighbour also laid out sod strips but rigged lights in some trees, shining on the new grass. The light kept away the raccoons, and the grass survived.

An idea for discouraging raccoons by the smell, which I have read about but not tried, is to place mason jars half full of bleach, with holes in the lids, at 10 to 14 foot intervals round the edge of the yard. Since this might lead to injuries to pets, it could be safer to bury the jars

THE NATURAL WORLD

to their necks to prevent them from being knocked over. Blood meal works for a night or so, but soon loses its effect.

I have a feeling that for some readers the last suggestion in this article will be the most interesting and useful: live and let live.

How Much Wood Would a Woodchuck Chuck?

October is the month when all good groundhogs in our area hibernate until April. They are sometimes called woodchucks, a corruption of *wuchak*, their Algonquian name. I was surprised to learn that the groundhog is a member of the squirrel family. Another surprise came from the American newspapers reporting "scumbags" stealing little American flags put out at the graves of war veterans in Hudson, New York. The "scumbags" turned out to be three-foot-tall groundhogs that used the flags to line their burrows for the comfort of their young, which they rear for about six weeks. The embarrassed officials decided to provide flagpoles too tall for a groundhog to reach.

To make their burrows, these little animals move about 3,500 pounds of soil (or about 35 cubic feet), digging down to five feet below ground level. They prefer to live their three to six years in the wild on the edges of woodlands. Groundhogs rarely rove far from their burrow entrance, living on grasses and other green plants growing nearby. Groundhogs will defend themselves when threatened, which is understandable, at which point their tail hairs stand up like a brush, from fear.

Over our 30-year tenure, we have observed successive groundhogs emerging from a hole at the base of the middle of three maple trees across from our kitchen window. We have never threatened them, and the groundhogs have developed unique personalities. One enjoyed sunbathing, stretched out on our front deck. Another liked to wander around sniffing (but not eating) the spring flowers, especially forget-me-nots, which come out under the trees out at the back.

According to Wikipedia, groundhogs can create a nuisance by burrowing under housing and in farmers' fields. I can honestly report that in 30 years we have never had a groundhog hole dug in the more open parts of our property or under our house. The only such hole I have seen was in an area of Toronto recently cleared and planted with acres of manicured lawns for a business park. The groundhog there looked thin and would not survive the winter.

Through long, bitter experience, wildlife avoid humans, unless forced into the open by our destruction of their habitat. Surely, if those businesses involving clear-cutting left wildlife some of the wooded areas and greenery for food and shelter that they need, the animals would only too willingly stay away from houses and ploughed land. People living in the new houses and near farms could enjoy this woodland, and all would benefit from better air quality provided by the trees. Also, farms would benefit from replacing some of the trees formerly cleared; to quote "Minto initiates new tree program" in the summer issue of *The Rural Route*, "Trees should be considered an important 'factor of production' on the farm, not just an amenity or show piece."

We ourselves live on a rural road with some farms, but mostly long-established properties that are not farmed. Some of the residential properties have been continuously occupied by the same family to the third generation. The properties are interspersed with wooded areas that run along sections of the Maitland River system. By custom and by law promoting good stewardship of our area for all the people and wildlife living there, further clear-cutting of trees is forbidden. Clear-cutting damages the air quality, warms the water thereby damaging water-based wildlife, and erodes the land near rivers.

If you have concerns about environmental or habitat destruction or pollution in your area, call your local Ministry of the Environment and/or Conservation Authority. To do their work effectively, these bodies rely on information from people on the spot.

The Maitland Valley Conservation Authority

We live on a rural property, which was severed in 1876, shortly after the area was settled. Like most of the properties on our part of the Sixth Line, it was designated as "residential non-farming" in the official plan. In many ways, the Maitland River and its tributaries dominate the land. Three of these cross our Line which joins the Seven Bridges Road (seven bridges across tributaries of the Maitland River). The creek running round our garden goes under a bridge and meanders through farms. The whole complex of rivers and tributaries is under the stewardship of the Maitland Valley Conservation Authority (MVCA).

Since 1951, this hard-working and rather low profile agency has joined with local municipalities to protect and improve area water, forest and soil resources. Their jurisdiction covers a wide swath from North Wellington, Mapleton and Perth East across to Lake Huron. As well as watershed stewardship, the MVCA has provided management services to some conservation areas, notably the Falls Reserve and Wawanesh Park.

In recent years, the climate here has featured more intense and localized thunderstorms than before. The MVCA provides two gauging stations to forecast flooding, and offers to local authorities training in dealing with such an event. In response to changes in the local climate, MVCA and their municipal partners have focussed their efforts particularly on reducing flooding and soil erosion, and on improving water quality by building watershed resiliency. Resiliency is defined as the ability of the watershed to smooth out the impacts of extremes of climate change (flooding and drought) and to deal with pests in order to preserve healthy forests, rivers and soil. For example, recently the MVCA prevented an installation which could have polluted our creek, groundwater and wells serving farm animals and over

HERE COMES THE MOON

20 people (mainly children). This could also have resulted in a ruinous drop in value of the affected properties.

Local newspapers have reported that this valuable authority is facing a financial crisis. Aging infrastructure, as well as funding fixed at the 1990 level, have forced the MVCA to reconsider its support of lesser used conservation areas. The municipal partners are in the midst of their own funding crunch. At a time when responding to climate change is crucial, efforts will have to be concentrated even more closely on flood control to minimize damage to town infrastructures, roads and buildings, and infrastructures and soil in rural areas.

To help stretch the budget, MVCA hopes for more volunteers. In this respect there is already an active volunteer organization in place: the Middle Maitland Rejuvenation Committee (MMRC). It requires more able-bodied helpers and also financial contributions. A registered charitable organization, the Maitland Conservation Foundation (MCF), works with MVCA to raise funds for conservation projects. Also, with MVCA advice, rural landowners can implement their own water quality projects, thus recognizing and facilitating their stewardship over the land they own.

We are fortunate to have the advice and actions of an organization such as the Maitland Valley Conservation Authority and should co-operate with it, and similar organizations in other areas, as much as possible.

Country Adventure

It started innocuously enough one fine September morning when my friend Beth and I set off on our bikes, each with a package of sandwiches, to go on a cycle run in the beautiful countryside of the poet Robert Burns outside the small town where we lived in Ayrshire, Scotland. In those days there were no six-lane straight highways bisecting the lush green fields and streams. These were given over to crops, and grass for the Ayrshire dairy cows, lovely soft brown- and cream-coloured animals famous for their agreeable temperament and high milk yield.

We had hardly begun our journey when we met our Phys. Ed. teacher Miss Angus walking along one of the narrow lanes edged with hedgerows. She was leading her horse. We stopped for a chat. Miss Angus said she was taking the horse to the local blacksmith to be re-shod.

Apart from enjoying the weather and countryside, Beth and I had a purpose. It was to harvest the exceptionally large chestnuts that right now would be lying under a tree on a farm. They would be perfect for conkers, a game we played in the school playground at recess. We soon came to a short-cut across a field that we had used before. Amblers were welcome to go across fields provided they obeyed the notice to "Please Close the Gate" tacked up on a piece of wood. So having dismounted from our bikes, Beth and I closed the gate behind us and wandered in a leisurely way across the small field towards the gate out of it. We pushed the bikes and talked companionably. However, about half way across, we became aware of a light vibrating of the ground behind us accompanied by a low, snorting sound.

We turned around to find ourselves being followed by a herd of the aforementioned lovely soft brown- and cream-coloured Ayrshire dairy cows famous for their agreeable temperament and high milk yield. In the lead was an Ayrshire bull, about whose temperament we were not so knowledgeable. Led by the bull the cattle, all with horns (in Scotland there is no de-horning), drifted apparently aimlessly towards us at a slow but increasing speed. Beth and I quickened our pace to a near run until we were close enough to the gate to make a dash for it. We threw our bikes against the gate and ourselves over it.

Turning round, we saw the bull about four feet from our bikes staring at us, at which point the cows took the opportunity to return to quietly chewing grass. After a few minutes, led by their bull the whole herd drifted off and my friend and I leaned over the gate to retrieve our bikes.

We collected our booty of conkers and sat down by a stream lined with primroses. (Yes, primroses in September: that's what I remember – and there are evening primroses that bloom all summer until frost.) In this idyllic setting Beth and I had the best sandwich lunch of that year.

We took the longer way home.

MAKING A DIFFERENCE

Author's Note (William of Malmesbury)

When I was eighteen and at university, I fell in love with an unusual older man who wrote beautifully. He had a large collection of books, and if he wanted one that was out of print, he borrowed a copy and reproduced it himself word-for-word, writing in an exquisite, small, medieval script. Unfortunately for me, *he* was medieval, having lived from about 1095–1153. His name was William and he was librarian of the English abbey of Malmesbury.

In the late seventh century BC, the scholar-poet Aldhelm founded Malmesbury Abbey under the Benedictine rule. William was from a wealthy and well-connected family, of mixed Norman and Saxon stock. He came as a seven-year-old to join under Abbot Godfrey. In the peaceful and orderly atmosphere of Malmesbury, William thrived; he made it his life's work to extend the already well-known and substantial library. Pursuing this aim, he turned down a promotion to Abbot at least twice. William was known for his good nature, endless patience and extraordinary industry.

Little is known of the details of William's life. However, as well as becoming a man of great learning, criticized by some for his knowledge of the pagan Greek, he was a respected historian. Some said William was a genius at history. He diligently sifted facts to find the truth.

William lived in that area of England where there was a strong interest in astronomy and astrology. His attitude to these subjects was ambiguous. He was against any dabbling in the occult. However, William respected his contemporary Robert of Hereford's successful astrological predictions, and was in favour of astronomy, but condemned superstition as working against man's free choice.

William was famous for his superior writing skills. Other religious houses such as Glastonbury competed to have William write their histories. For his time, he was a very original writer. William varied his writing style to suit the subject, and portrayed character by starting

HERE COMES THE MOON

with a few facts and gradually building it up. He also varied his material (factual, legends, going from home to an event abroad etc.). His writing style could be read easily (in translation from the Latin) today. William's small and perfectly formed handwriting is evocative of his meticulous approach. There is an example of it in Westminster Cathedral, London, England.

When William started his final illness in the late 1130s, he wrote the accounts of the Marian miracles. William put his stories of miracles in the order of the importance of those benefitting, in the world of his *own* day. Bishops and abbots came first, then monks, clerks, priests, laymen and lastly women and images. This shows his brilliant grasp of history, and understanding of how things could change. The final epilogue was in the form of a prayer to the Virgin written as if he expected to die soon.

Fortunately for me, however, at the same time I also fell in love with a contemporary young man, a fellow student. We married, and now live by a stream, among Mennonite farms in southwestern Ontario. There, we were at one time regularly visited by barn cats, one of whom, a very small female, became a particular friend. The following piece is a setting of that little cat with William in the cloisters of Malmesbury.

Scene with Cat in Malmesbury Abbey

The cat gave a delicate lick to her paws and started to wash her face. Next, she reared up and worked down her front, revealing two diamond-shaped markings, bright white against the black of her other fur. The fastidious creature cleaned off traces of the straw on which she had been sleeping the previous night.

At a bench along the wall of the cloisters, two elderly monks played checkers on a board carved into the wood; under the cool arches William paused in his work for the scriptorium and smiled at the sight of the little cat in a characteristic feline pose, her hind leg pointed straight up as she washed her nether regions. The endearing white dot of fur at the end of her outstretched tail shone in the sun.

Although not one of the monastery cats, she came to visit William every day.

Not long after she first appeared, he happened to drop a stylus just behind where she was sitting, and she didn't even look round. William knew she would not respond if he called, for the creature was deaf.

When the cat, fully-grown but tiny, first came to visit, she had been happy to sit peacefully by herself. Even when William brought food, she would not allow him to come near, but ate only when he had walked away a few yards. Gradually though, the little animal had become more confident. Shr ran up when she saw William, rolling over for him to stroke her front.

William left one of his assistants to continue the manuscript he was copying and went to sit on a bench in the cloister garden. His mind wandered back to memories of childhood in his aristocratic father's large house. William had so enjoyed the lessons in French and Latin and calligraphy – and quietly endured the bullying (teasing she called it) of his older sister who was not interested in her letters. William had retaliated in a typical manner: by writing in the margin of one of his father's many books "Margery ys a shrewe."

What a joy it had been for seven-year-old William to enter the calm cloister of Malmesbury Abbey and be set to helping Abbot Godfrey with the library. Ever since, he had devoted himself to expanding its holdings, twice refusing a promotion to abbot. It had been a good life – no, *wonderful* – travelling to other monasteries in search of new books to copy and add to the Malmesbury holdings.

William remembered how he had marvelled at the English countryside, enjoying its rich beauty at all times of year. He remembered trees, floating in the January mist, the sun a silver coin in the sky. Riding along in summer, William could pick a ripe apple off a wayside tree. And then there was the bounty of autumn, when the light of the rising sun was so golden all over that he could barely distinguish the stooks of wheat waiting to be threshed. It was on such an autumn morning that he had first noticed the little black cat, distinct against the yellow, making her way over the hard stubble, limping to protect her injured leg.

Amidst the upsurge of interest in astronomy, astrology and even the occult by William's contemporaries, William remembered taking a stern stand against the latter. However, he respected the successful divinations of Robert of Hereford. His own calling had been to build a magnificent library at Malmesbury. In doing so, William had turned to writing the History both of the Church and of England. His family connections provided an insider's knowledge of the more recent history and important people involved. (An interest in ordinary people was yet to come.) He had meticulously researched the historical facts that he could find and was pleased with the result.

William's original writing style and the eminence he achieved as a historian had put him in high demand for writing the histories of other religious houses. As a result William had been able to take refuge in Glastonbury for six years. He seemed to remember leaving Malmesbury early in 1129 and returning in mid-1135. By leaving Malmesbury, he was typically avoiding, rather than confronting, potential disagreements with Bishop Roger of Salisbury, then overlord of Malmesbury.

William did not feel his life had been narrow. Rather his life had been one of varied experiences, not all spent in obscurity in libraries. He had attended the 1141 Council of Winchester when Matilda was acknowledged Lady of England. There, he had witnessed the behind-the-scenes plotting of the barons (through his father William knew

MAKING A DIFFERENCE

them all) about whether to keep their promise to her father. These promises had been made during the troubled times of civil war with her cousin Stephen over who should rule. Rulers come and they go. William was happy to have spent his life's work on books, which survive. By now, William had completed his massive histories of the English church and state and recently a history of the Marian miracles. In a final epilogue prayer to the Virgin, he had acknowledged his illness and approaching death; his soul was at peace.

In the warmth of the rising sun, the cloister garden had slipped out of its filmy covering of mist. Soothed by the subdued splashing of a fountain, William thought of the symbolic nature of the lilies and roses before him: the white of lilies signifying the purity of the Virgin, the red of roses a sign for the blood and martyrdom of Christ.

Bees, droning methodically from flower to flower before returning to their hives in the herb garden, were not concerned about the flowers' religious symbolism. Neither was the cat, relaxed away from the life-and-death battles of her community in the barn on the neighbouring farm. Shutting her eyes, the creature yawned, showing white teeth and a pink tongue in sharp contrast to the black of her neatly rounded head.

Clean at last, she sat in the sun, narrowing her yellow eyes and hunching her shoulders in dreamy appreciation of the surroundings. Earlier that morning, after Prime, William had fed her. The tiny cat was content.

Poem to William of Malmesbury

Versed in Latin, French and English
A weary, seven-year-old boy toils
Helping Abbot Godfrey in the
Library and scriptorium

Riding out to monasteries
Discovering books to collect
Tireless, copying manuscripts
In exquisite calligraphy

Refusing the post of abbot
In his quest to write history,
And write well, explaining his craft
To generations yet to come

Last work: Marian miracles
Listed in order of value –
Then – (women and images last)
Tells us of his final illness

For us to reach back and cure him?
Constantly he held us in mind
His whole oeuvre a cry of longing
Down the ages, "Remember me."

Joyfully Towards Eighty-one We Go!

Recently, I and my cohort of friends from high school and beyond were surprised to reach our eightieth birthdays: Already? How could eighty years have gone by so quickly?

We're certainly the same people we ever were, but with some modifications. We're broader in the beam, and broader in our tolerance of others and their ideas. Yes, the joints are stiff, but the mind is more flexible, and will consider alternatives. Slower movements and more time after retirement allow us to think about issues more deeply, develop better balanced opinions than before, enter discussions without anger. There's the space to extend our horizons, to relax and be ourselves, feel joy and wonder at simple things, like the view out of a kitchen window, the local wildlife, fir trees under a new fall of snow – something we sometimes lost in the over busy middle years.

The hearing is less acute, but the ability to really listen to what others have to say has expanded. Patience has developed that wasn't there before, and a better acceptance of the aches and pains we must bear. We have reached the calm, sure love of long commitment.

Death, a reality we never even considered in younger years, is now a certainty – but not so near that we cannot still achieve something new, laugh at a joke, and go forward in good cheer.

So joyfully towards eighty-one we go.

Agnes Macphail

Proton Township Farmer's Daughter – Agnes Macphail

On March, 24, 1890, a child was born on a farm in Proton Township of Ontario's Grey County, the eldest of three daughters. Then, women did not have the status of "persons" in Canada. However, by the time she was in her thirties that had changed. By then, this lady's opinions were reported in newspapers across North America and Britain, and she was much in demand as a speaker continent-wide. As the first woman member of the Canadian House of Commons, the farmer's daughter accomplished an enormous amount for her constituency of farmers, and in the field of social progress.

A bronze bust of her is now displayed near the Speaker's Chambers in the (Canadian) House of Commons. Several schools (one in Flesherton) bear her name, and in a 2005 province-wide competition she was voted the Greatest Ontario Woman. By now you will have guessed who she was: Agnes Macphail. The Toronto-based Agnes Macphail Recognition Committee gives an annual award for outstanding contributions in the areas of equal rights, social justice and leadership.

The early 1900s were hard times for farming, a calling that Agnes later characterized as one of "bent backs, callused hands and limited rewards ... the most arduous and most poorly paid of all occupations."

Agnes had excelled in her schoolwork, and after a two-year break to help on the farm, at sixteen was on her way to the highly regarded Owen Sound Collegiate, where one of her fellow students was Norman Bethune, also destined for later fame. At Owen Sound, because of her country clothes and country way of speaking, at first Agnes Macphail had difficulties fitting in. However, her high achievement at her studies soon had the other girls asking her to help them with their homework. From Owen Sound Agnes moved to Stratford where she had friends at the Normal School there, and graduated as a teacher. Although

HERE COMES THE MOON

offered positions in towns, Agnes Macphail chose to teach in several country schools.

For many women during that time, a career as a teacher would have been the end of the story. However, through her landlord, Agnes became aware of broad concerns affecting farmers, and she also developed a considerable expertise on the issue of tariffs; so much so, that in December, 1919, she was one of several delegates from the United Farmers Organization (UFO) presenting to the Tariff Commission headed by the federal Minister of finance.

Times were changing in rural Canada. The UFO was working to send some of its own people to represent farmers' interests in Parliament. But who among them would have the public-speaking skills?

During Sam Foote's campaign for North York, Agnes, who had demonstrated a talent for public speaking, had been asked to speak on behalf of the inarticulate Sam. She described him as "the farmeriest farmer I ever saw." Soon, Agnes was addressing thousands of farmers and their wives who had converged by horse and buggy on the Durham arena, and later Durham's town hall. There, on September, 26, 1921, she was chosen by 150 UFO delegates to run as the UFO candidate for South East Grey. Agnes's campaign speeches across the riding brought out further thousands to listen. When she ended her speeches by restating the UFO motto "Equal rights to all and special privileges to none" the cheers for "Our Aggie" (respectfully addressed as "Miss Macphail" in public) might have stampeded the horses outside if they had not been so firmly tethered.

In her private life, Agnes Macphail was enormous fun: visits from her were accompanied by gales of laughter. Up until then, Agnes had lived a secure life with family and friends, people she never forgot, always keeping in touch with "My Ain Folk" (the title of her autobiography). Just before the election, her adored maternal grandmother, Jean Campbell, died at the age of 91; Agnes Macphail had to face the next stage of her career without her grandmother's strong support.

A taste of what was in store could be found in the reaction of the press. The election of Canada's first woman MP made the front pages of newspapers in the United States and was received ecstatically in Grey County. However, this historic fact was noted only on the sixth page of the *Toronto Globe* under the heading of "Old Faces and New", a chilling hint of what was to come.

38

MAKING A DIFFERENCE

After an initial show of welcome, the bitter resentment and relentless opposition of almost all male members of Parliament set in. (Notable exceptions were J. S. Woodsworth and Ernest Lapointe.) Even the other women in Ottawa resented Agnes; she was not, for instance, invited to a banquet for the British MP the Duchess of Atholl. The Duchess complained; so Prime Minister King arranged a private lunch with Agnes. Of her early years in Parliament, Agnes wrote: "Perhaps if I owed him [father Dugald] the ability to get into Parliament, I owed her [mother Henrietta] the ability to stand it."

This hostility was accompanied by a critical press – even from other women. One journalist described her as "not exactly lovable." A large daily jeered, "Progressives have no love for Grits or Tories, declared Miss Agnes Macphail in Toronto. Does Agnes know what love is?"

From the perspective of her private life, Agnes certainly did know love. She had already received proposals of marriage from distinguished suitors in Grey County and was soon wooed by fellow MPs Preston Elliott and Robert Gardiner. Prime Minister R. B. Bennett later proposed. However, there was always the problem of equality (or rather inequality) in marriage. It made Agnes draw back from that commitment.

Agnes took her public position seriously, soon learning to defend herself and make her point. In debate she developed a bitter sarcasm and biting wit. Agnes also lost her less polished look and became well dressed, in a tailored way, while on most public duties. Her beautiful, low speaking voice reached all parts of the House of Commons. Wilfred Eggleston, director of Carleton College School of Journalism, said, "She lit into people in a way to rip their hide." It was just as well that Agnes was no pushover, as she was also years ahead of her male colleagues in her views on social issues, which she soon took up as well as continuing her aim of benefitting farmers.

Agnes quickly bettered the condition of agriculture by having tariffs lowered and enabling farmers to market produce at fairer prices. These actions helped those not only in Ontario, but also across Canada. Western grain growers could now choose where to store and ship their grain.

When issues came forward in Parliament, this practical farmer's daughter went to see for herself. In 1925, when the miners of Glace Bay went on strike against a reduction in pay, instead of merely reading the self-serving reports of the British Empire Steel Corporation and its

HERE COMES THE MOON

supporters, Agnes Macphail travelled to where the miners worked. First hand, she found out they had been kept short of work for four years and could not clothe and feed their families, who lived in shacks with deplorable sanitary conditions. This led to a debate in Parliament and later action. Like many other rookie members of parliament, Agnes Macphail was surprised at the slow pace of the Parliamentary process.

She also insisted on touring Kingston Penitentiary to see at first-hand the condition of the prisoners there. After being refused entry as a woman, Agnes obtained it using her status as a member of Parliament. She saw the beatings with a leather strap, which had holes to tear out the skin, and men in shackles and in solitary confinement. Agnes started the first Elizabeth Fry Society in Canada and through perseverance against bitter opposition, brought about prison reform such as paid work for prisoners and other benefits. These changes brought down the 72 percent rate of recidivism. Some of the prison reforms she proposed, such as an end to solitary confinement, have still not been legislated.

Canada's first woman MP, also the first female member of the League of Nations' Disarmament Committee, worked for world peace and, at home, proposed substituting gymnastics programs for those of military training for boys in the schools. With others, she changed the *laissez faire* attitude of Canadians to one of understanding that the whole nation was collectively responsible for the welfare of all its citizens from youth to old age.

Agnes Macphail was a one-person whirlwind, privately helping the poor and desperate out of her own pocket. Agnes also helped handi-capped people and war veterans and their families to obtain pensions, and advocated for health care and the rights of women, in particular over divorce settlements. To address the problem of goitre, common in Grey County, Agnes Macphail successfully petitioned parliament to have iodine added to table salt.

Though she suffered recurring health problems, Agnes financed her personal charity by becoming a sought after public speaker throughout Canada and especially the United States, where her status as Canada's first woman MP was praised. Despite her health and financial con-cerns, Agnes was still pursued by men who wanted her in marriage (there are ardent love letters in the National Archives).

Given the high profile Agnes had achieved as a public speaker and MP, she was by now hobnobbing with the rich and famous – in the

40

MAKING A DIFFERENCE

United States with the likes of Henry Ford, and in Canada with major movers and shakers, including Nellie McClung who was also born in southwestern Ontario. However, Agnes Macphail did not forget her constituents. Agnes sent weekly letters, found funding for Durham Post Office, and provided social events, writing and public-speaking competitions for young people, with a trip to Ottawa as the prize – all paid for out of her own pocket.

In what was to be Agnes Macphail's last term in Parliament she achieved the most of any term, and what many see as Agnes's crowning achievement: prison reform via the 1939 Penitentiary Bill brought in by the new minister of justice, one of her few MP supporters, Ernest Lapointe. Partly due to terrible weather, which kept her older supporters from the polls, Agnes Macphail lost the 1940 election. She rose again politically, this time as one of the first two female Ontario MPPs. In that position, Agnes was instrumental in obtaining equal pay legislation for the province in 1951.

Agnes Macphail suffered two strokes and died in 1954, just short of both her 64th birthday and a Senate appointment. Agnes Macphail's last written communication about herself was to the *Canadian Encyclopedia*. Under "Special Honours" Agnes wrote: "No special honours except the love of people, which I value more than any other."

Agnes was buried beside her parents in Priceville, Grey County. Typically, her funeral was accompanied by extreme weather. Among the wreaths was one from the Inmates' Welfare Committee of Kingston Penitentiary. The "In Memoriam" for Agnes in their newsletter stated: "The changes wrought within these cold grey walls were her handiwork; to her must go our tribute."

At the funeral, the church minister said that Agnes Campbell Macphail had "returned with honour to the county in which she was born … There had been little good social legislation in the past 30 years in which Agnes Macphail had not had a considerable part … She was a friend of the weak, champion of the underprivileged and a protector of the unfortunate." This was a fitting farewell for a truly great lady.

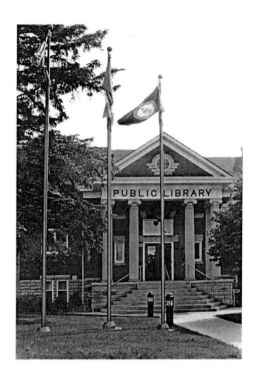

Public Library, Harriston

Carnegie Libraries

Recently, two Carnegie libraries in our area of southwestern Ontario, at Harriston and Mt. Forest, have been renovated and expanded, with a third, at Palmerston, on its way. Of the 125 such libraries in Canada, 111 were built in Ontario. As well as Harriston, Mt. Forest and Palmerston, the Listowel, Lucknow and Teeswater libraries are also Carnegies. They are named after Andrew Carnegie, a Scottish-American businessman who by the time he died in 1919 had financed over 2,500 libraries, most of them in North America and Britain.

Who was Andrew Carnegie – and why was he so interested in setting up libraries with free access for the general public?

This exceptional man was born in 1835 at Dunfermline, Scotland. His father, William (Will), was a poor weaver and, according to his son, "a most lovable man ... not a man of the world, and a man all over for heaven." Will Carnegie helped start the Tradesman's Subscription Library in Dunfermline and instilled in his son a love of learning, of debate and figures (leading to Andrew's knowledge of accounting). Mother Margaret (Mag) was made of sterner stuff. She helped put food on the family table by binding shoes for local master shoemakers, and she encouraged her son in all his entrepreneurial ambitions. Both these influences were crucial to Andrew Carnegie's future success.

After immigrating to Pittsburgh, Pennsylvania, at the age of 13, he soon found a job, deliberately lost his Scottish accent and began climbing the ladder in increasingly responsible telegrapher positions. At 18 he became assistant to Thomas Scott, the senior telegrapher of Pennsylvania Railroad. There he learned about the railroads and about business in general. At the age of 21 Andrew Carnegie was appointed Superintendent. On his way up, at the age of 17, Andrew Carnegie fought successfully for the right of working boys like himself to obtain books free from the Anderson subscription library in Pittsburgh.

HERE COMES THE MOON

By the time he was 35, this diminutive man, who always sought to disguise his lack of height by wearing high-heeled boots and top hats in public, was living in grand style with his mother in New York (father Will having died when his son was 20). From New York, always keeping a firm eye on the accounting records, Andrew Carnegie ran his Homestead steel mills in Pittsburgh through managers such as his brother Tom, Henry Clay Frick and Charles Schwab.

It was through his comparative analysis of industry financial statistics that Carnegie realized that his workers were earning more than others in the steel industry and working less (eight hours a day instead of twelve). He decided that with better financial management, the Carnegie mills could be even more profitable.

The imposition of lower wages and longer working hours led to a round of strikes – broken by the managers. Carnegie counselled his workers that if they wanted improved conditions, they must work through their union to obtain them, but for the industry as a whole not just for themselves. Andrew Carnegie had successfully imposed on his workers the working standards of the other "robber barons" of his time and in so doing had increased his already huge profits.

This accumulation of wealth led to the question of how to "return the profits to the community from which they came" – as Carnegie put it. (He did not consider his workers as being part of that community.) Early in his career, Andrew Carnegie had decided to give away, during his lifetime and in a responsible way, all the money he made. *Forbes* magazine estimated this, in 2007 dollars, at almost $300 billion by the height of his success.

Carnegie advised his workers to take an interest in reading and relaxing games in their (now much reduced) spare time. He turned a blind eye to the terrible living conditions of his now poorer workers, and to the fact that working 12 hours a day seven days a week gave them little time or energy for leisure pursuits. However, these were different times from the admittedly difficult ones he had himself encountered coming to America. It is no surprise that the working masses of Pittsburgh urged their local authority not to request or accept the gift of a library from such a man. However, the city politicians answered that Carnegie had the money, they didn't, and that they may as well get back some of it.

The libraries were not a completely free gift. Cities had to prove a need, donate a building site, assign annual taxes to support the library,

MAKING A DIFFERENCE

and promise to provide the library's services absolutely free to their citizens. Library members were to have access to browse in the stacks and choose books.

As time went by, Andrew Carnegie met Louise Whitfield, a young woman of old and respectable New York lineage. They married in 1886 after the death of his mother. At the dinner parties Louise hosted, Andrew displayed his scintillating conversational skills. He loved his wife too dearly to go ahead with having a family; in those days, it was common for a woman to die in childbirth. However, Louise pined for a child, and in March, 1897, their much loved daughter, named Margaret after Andrew's mother, was born when Andrew was 62 and Louise just turning 40.

Before the wedding, Louise had signed an agreement giving her an annual income of $3 million in today's dollars, and renouncing any claim on her husband's larger estate, which she would help him to disburse. Later, the donations of the Carnegie fortune were entrusted to another Scot, Carnegie's secretary James Bertram, who dispensed money mainly for educational and scientific enterprises. When Bertram died he was not buried in the United States, but with his wife in her birthplace in Canada: Seaforth, Ontario.

By the end of his life, Andrew Carnegie, who by now mixed with all the most powerful world leaders, became obsessed with bringing about world peace. He died of pneumonia in 1919, disappointed that this initiative had obviously failed. Andrew Carnegie was not accustomed to failing at anything.

Nellie McClung

Nellie McClung

Like Agnes Macphail, Nellie McClung was born in Grey County (Chatsworth) to a farming family, but she was born in 1873, seventeen years earlier than Agnes. When Nellie was seven, they moved west to what was then the more fertile soil of Manitoba. Also like Agnes, Nellie was a "handful" for her family to manage, always ready with a joke or to mimic older people – and desperate to obtain an education, which she started at the late age of ten. Nellie's excellent teacher, Mr. Schulz, taught her to read in a few months. He also taught her to question the status quo. From then on, there was no stopping Nellie. She soon became a teacher in rural schools and started writing articles for local papers. It was during this period that Nellie met her future mother-in-law and mentor, Annie McClung, and then Wes McClung, Annie's son, a successful pharmacist who soon married Nellie.

A year later, the first of their five children was born. Nellie had live-in help and continued to write, bringing out a best-selling book *Sewing Seeds in Denny,* with its feisty heroine Pearlie Watson. This led to many lucrative speaking engagements. Like Agnes Macphail after her, Nellie proved to be an engaging and witty public speaker, which brought her contact with leading women such as Cora E. Hind of Winnipeg, an accurate forecaster of the wheat yield, and a member of the Canadian Women's Press Club. Cora would later play an important role in Nellie's life.

Also like Agnes, Nellie paid careful attention to her appearance and always had a fashionable outfit for speaking engagements. With the support of Wes, and help in the house, Nellie was able to keep very much abreast of her family's concerns, and to guide her children in their lives. Throughout her life, Nellie's door was always open to them, and to others seeking advice,

Nellie became concerned about the condition of farm women, worn out by long hours of work and little money, in some cases due

HERE COMES THE MOON

to their husbands drinking it away. She joined the Women's Christian Temperance Union (WCTU). Influenced by her mother-in-law, Nellie also began to support women's suffrage. She ended all her speeches with a plea for suffrage, using as her spokesperson Pearlie Watson, the well-known character from her book, *Sewing Seeds in Denny*.

Wes's new insurance job took the family to Winnipeg, where Nellie thrived, joining many women's organizations and renewing her friendship with Cora Hind. There, Nellie not only enjoyed the larger opportunities for reading and attendance at plays and recitals, but also took time to see the terrible conditions of working immigrant women in sweatshops. These women's children were left to fend for themselves in hovels. She and her friend Mrs Claude Nash persuaded the premier Sir Rodmond Roblin to go and see for himself. His view was that these women lived at home and worked for pin money, and something to do. After seeing the actual sweatshops, Roblin said he could not understand "why two women like you should ferret out such utterly disgusting things."

Premier Roblin had similarly old-fashioned views on women's suffrage, which he said was supported by "short-haired women and long-haired men.""Nice women do not want the vote," he said.

Nellie McClung decided to fight for her causes, not by indignation and violence as had the British suffragettes, but through building contacts with women's organizations, and trying to change public opinion by publicity and with humour. The women held mock parliaments in theatres, with Nellie mimicking Premier Roblin. The audiences not only had a rollicking good time, but also came away converted. In 1915, the new Liberal government of Manitoba took up the causes and by early 1916 brought in both prohibition and the franchise for women.

Soon, Wes's work transferred the family to Edmonton, Alberta, where Nellie again took up the cudgels. With the help of other women, notably Emily Murphy and Alice Jamieson, the first two female magistrates in the British Empire, she successfully lobbied the legislature to bring in prohibition and female suffrage for Alberta. The first month after prohibition, in 1924, drunkenness convictions fell by 80 percent and household savings rose by 100 percent. Votes for women soon followed in the other provinces.

After going to Edmonton, in 1915 Nellie McClung wrote *In Times Like These*, now recognized as a key Canadian statement of first wave feminism.

MAKING A DIFFERENCE

The period after the First World War saw Nellie disappointed that there had been a loss of momentum in the progress for women. Far from encouraging women to accomplish more with their expanded spare time, the new labour-saving devices had ushered in the era of the bored, neurotic housewife.

Nellie propelled herself forward, and in 1921, the same year that Agnes Macphail became the first woman MP, she entered politics as a Liberal MLA. Although she believed in working through established parties rather than the newer "fringe" ones, as did Agnes Macphail, Nellie could not confine herself to the ideas of one party. She joined the only other female MLA, Conservative Irene Parlby, in supporting equal treatment for women in divorce, and in opposing the idea that women married to a wage earner should not earn a wage themselves.

After her defeat in the 1926 election, Nellie McClung confined herself to her writing and felt better able to lobby for her views from outside any legislature. With like-minded women, Nellie continued to advocate equal treatment for all people in Canada, especially the Métis, First Nations and immigrant groups subjected to discrimination, such as the Chinese and Japanese Canadians. When, during the Second World War, the latter were interned, she made sure education continued for the children through the provincial education services. The women's pleas for sanctuary in Canada for Jewish people, or at the very least for their children, were unsuccessful.

However, many things did change, notably the climate of opinion in Canada. This brought in mother's allowances, school nurses, travelling libraries, help for immigrants in learning English and later the establishment of a national health service and the 1967 Royal Commission on the Status of Women in Canada.

As she aged, Nellie McClung's health deteriorated and she was stricken by arthritis and heart disease. After 1926 her days of achievement in the public sphere were over, and Nellie was not sorry to take a peaceful and happy retirement with Wes on the west coast in the house they christened Lantern Lane. A lantern was always lit to guide people to it, and many still came to see Nellie, who died there in September, 1951 aged 78.

There was, however, one shining exception: the famous Person's Case (1929) the culmination of a move taken by five women (a minimum of five people was required) to change the British North America (BNA) Act. To allow women to take their place in Canada's

HERE COMES THE MOON

Senate, they had to be recognized as "persons" along with men. The five women, funded by Justice Minister Ernest Lapointe, were Emily Murphy, Irene Parlby, Louise McKinney (president of the WCTU), Nellie McClung and Henrietta Muir Edwards, co-founder of the National Council of Women. They are now known as The Famous Five. The case failed in Canada's Supreme Court, but succeeded on appeal to the Judicial Committee of the Privy Council in Britain, where Lord Sankey declared that "the exclusion of women from all public offices is a relic of days more barbarous than ours." He said that the BNA Act was "a living tree capable of growth and expansion within its natural limits."

The still celebrated achievement of the Famous Five is commemorated by a statue of the Famous Five in Winnipeg, a plaque in the Parliament Buildings and by a statue of the women on Parliament Hill, Ottawa, with an identical one in Calgary. Among the Calgary and Ottawa statues, the fashionably clad woman waving a copy of the decision is Nellie McClung.

Chad Martin of Palmerston –
How One Thing Led to Another

Chad Martin's grandmother was born and raised in Wallace Township. She spent most of her life working and raising a family on a small farm. When he was 19, Chad's grandmother handed him a suitcase full of family photographs and other memorabilia. She also gave him some family heirlooms as she felt he would take care of them. I wonder whether his grandmother fully realized what she was starting. By the time Chad was in his late twenties, one thing had led to another and with his father's active encouragement Chad became addicted to collecting. But this was not just any kind of collecting.

At first, his interest took the form of finding family pictures and postcards. Chad even found a postcard featuring the creamery where his mother worked. In his address on January, 17, 2015 at the Wellington County Museum, Chad recalled fond memories of visiting his mother at the end of her work day to accompany her home, with a treat from the creamery to eat on the way. Chad's favourite was chocolate milk.

With this card not strictly from his family, Chad's love of his family began to expand to the love he felt for his hometown. Soon the collection contained many postcards, calendars and pictures of Palmerston. During his talk Chad showed a photograph of the main street of Palmerston taken a century ago. He pointed out that it hasn't changed much since then. One charming snap of Chad as a child, standing on the old 81 steam engine, was followed by the information that, in a continuation of his family tradition, he takes photos of his children posed in the same way on the same engine in the new railway park in Palmerston.

During the address, Chad's love shone through for his family and their hometown, according to Chad pronounced "Pammerstun" by those over 45 and "Palmerston" by those under that age. Chad Martin's

HERE COMES THE MOON

talk was full of fascinating extra information, for instance that people applied the designation "palmer" to those who had been on a pilgrimage to the Holy Land, returning from their journey with a palm frond. As time went by, the collection of pictures and other memorabilia increased to over 300 items of any type of art and paper documents. One of these is the January 20, 1875, minutes of the first Palmerston Town Council meeting after its incorporation. The minutes were written in the strikingly beautiful copperplate handwriting of that era, now long replaced (since 1917) by typing.

The collection includes calendars, which became especially popular in the 1950s, and postcards. Chad pointed out the interesting nature not only of the cards, but of the messages on the back: telling of a journey interrupted in Palmerston, or a trip planned, even a joke or two about the town itself. However, Palmerston is a self-confident, close-knit community that can take a joke, and likes a good laugh.

The interest in collecting items related to the Martin family and Palmerston soon extended to finding historical facts about the town itself and then the whole area of southwestern Ontario where Palmerston is located. Chad gave an engrossing summary of past events, starting with a picture of a basic log cabin in the wilderness. He discussed the difficulties faced by the original settlers in travelling long distances for food and other supplies and then cooking and keeping clean. In addition to clearing the land, settlers had to build a road along a 66-foot frontage of their property, using logs split in half lengthwise and laid end to end. Because of their resemblance in appearance to the fabric, these were called "corduroy" roads.

Better times came with the extension of the Wellington, Grey and Bruce Railway across to Palmerston, causing a jump in population from 350 in 1873 to 1,693 in 1874. Since then Palmerston has had its ups and downs, but there has never been any question of its being abandoned and becoming a ghost town. The people of Palmerston have stayed and the town has survived. This excellent exhibit runs until May 10, 2015, at the Wellington County Museum on County Road 18 between Fergus and Elora. It is well worth a visit or two.

What is even more impressive about Chad (as well as his collection) is the fact that he has determined to extend his giving back to his community to publicizing it abroad. Chad's recently established blog on Facebook, No One Goes 2 Palmerston Ontario (taken from the Palmerston postal code: N0G 2P0) has already drawn over 700 friends

MAKING A DIFFERENCE

from Canada, and other places in the English-speaking world such as Ireland and even Australia.

Also, Chad Martin has turned his attention to geocaching, which has become popular over many countries since Dave Ulmer of Beavercreek, Oregon (USA) placed the first cache on May 3, 2000. Using a GPS or mobile device, seekers can find a small, waterproof book in which they sign their name or code name and replace the book. Thanks to Chad Martin there are now seven geocache locations in Palmerston. Add this to his blog's burgeoning presence on Facebook, and who knows, Palmerston could become a point of travel interest across Canada and even the world, with corresponding benefits for the Minto area.

There appears to be no end to this enterprising young man's vision. Fairly soon this year (2015), Chad is launching a website: www.noonegoes.com. We'll all have to look out for it.

To answer the original question, when Chad Martin's grandmother handed him the suitcase of family memorabilia, it's unlikely that she could possibly have realized what she was starting.

John McCrae

John McCrae – poet, artist, soldier and doctor

Few people could deserve these many designations so well as Canada's famous John McCrae. May, 2015 is the one-hundredth anniversary of the world renowned "In Flanders Fields", written on the deaths of members of the same brigade, Lieutenants Owen Hague and Alexis Helmer. The deaths of these popular young men probably inspired the poem, published December, 8, 1915 in the British magazine *Punch*. "In Flanders Fields" has received so much of the spotlight, that for a balanced picture of John McCrae it seems reasonable now to pause and remember what he was like as a person, and his other achievements, which have tended to fade into the background.

Most certainly, from the time he wrote his first poem as a high school student in Guelph, Ontario, John McCrae was a poet. At the age of 16, he was the first Guelph student to win a scholarship to the University of Toronto. While completing two degrees there, John McCrae had 16 of his 30 poems and several short stories published in magazines such as *Saturday Night*. Throughout John's lifetime, he continued to write and be published. Like "In Flanders Fields" many of these poems reflected John's life experiences, as did the talented entries in his sketchbook. Perhaps presciently, an 1886 entry is a sketch of poppies.

During John's many travels abroad and in Canada, and in his beloved outdoors world, John continued to draw, never allowing recurring asthma attacks to slow the pursuit of his many interests. During the medical career in Montreal in the early 1900s John McCrae, a gregarious man, was a member of the Pen and Pencil Club – set up to promote arts and letters in Montreal – where he became friends with the painter A. Y. Jackson and fellow writer Stephen Leacock. At the same time, John McCrae was also a member of the (literary) Shakespeare Club in Toronto, one of whose original members had been the painter Cornelius Krieghoff. Shortly before the club

HERE COMES THE MOON

transferred from Montreal to Toronto, Krieghoff painted a delightful portrait dated 1847 of the current members, including himself.

Severe asthma attacks led John to leave the University of Toronto temporarily to teach as assistant resident master at the Ontario Agricultural College in Guelph. While at the University of Toronto, he met Alice McRae, sister of a classmate. Both John's sketches and writing took a turn to sadness when Alice died of typhoid at the early age of 19. Her death greatly affected him. Nevertheless, John persevered at the University of Toronto where he completed a BA (1894) and an MD (1898). John McCrae paid for his medical studies by tutoring other students. He achieved so well in his own studies that the Faculty of Medicine awarded him a medal.

Artist, poet and doctor, this was an attractive man much sought after for social events. While later at university in Toronto, John McCrae wrote his mother about attending a YMCA party with 70 gentlemen and only ten ladies there. John had talked to all the ladies and been asked to escort one of them home. During the Boer War in which he fought, John McCrae developed a firm friendship with the head of nursing sisters, Margaret McDonald, describing her in another letter to his mother as "a mighty good sort" (no romance there). John was attracted to the French singing coach Beatriz D'Arniero who however married a Guelph opera singer, Edward Johnson. Still rather unlucky in love, though there were other friends such as Laura Kains of Guelph with whom he corresponded, John McCrae was very much regarded as an eligible bachelor by party givers. He next fell in love with Nona Gwyn, younger sister of his brother Tom's wife, and asked her to marry him. She turned John down, and despite his many attractions, John never married. His life was cut off too soon.

His own medical problem and those of others such as Alice McRae may have turned this multi-talented man towards the study of medicine. After graduation, John McCrae first became a resident house officer at Toronto General Hospital, and later joined Johns Hopkins Hospital in Baltimore, Maryland. There he worked with his brother Thomas, also a doctor, and with fellow Canadian Sir William Osler.

After fighting in the South African War John completed his fellowship in pathology at McGill University, then became resident pathologist at Montreal General Hospital; he later became assistant pathologist at the Royal Victoria Hospital also in Montreal. At the same time, John was professor of pathology at the University of Vermont. By 1904

MAKING A DIFFERENCE

he was off on his travels again, and spent several months working and studying in Britain, where John became a member of the Royal College of Physicians.

While continuing to work and teach at several hospitals, in 1905 John McCrae set up his own practice. Also in 1905, he became pathologist to the Montreal Foundling and Baby Hospital; in 1908 John was appointed physician to the Royal Alexandra Hospital for Infectious Diseases. Until 1911, he continued teaching at the University of Vermont. John and his brother Thomas, a distinguished doctor who had continued at Johns Hopkins Hospital, made major contributions to Osler's *Modern Medicine*, a 10-volume textbook published in 1909. In 1912, with J. George Adami, John McCrae co-authored *A Text-Book of Pathology for Students of Medicine*. This textbook was widely adopted and in 1914 went into a second, revised, edition. Adami described John as the most talented physician of his generation.

During these frantically busy years he attended and read papers at medical conferences in Europe and wrote articles for the *Montreal Medical Journal* and *American Journal of Medical Science*. The many friends John McCrae made socially included Governor General Lord Grey who asked him to be expedition physician for a canoeing trip from Norway House on Lake Winnipeg to Hudson's Bay. John knew how to balance work and leisure.

Born into the second generation of a successful Scottish Presbyterian immigrant family with a strong military background – his father was Lieutenant Colonel David McCrae – John joined the Highfield Cadet Corps at the age of 14. When he was 17, he enlisted in the Militia Field Battery commanded by his father and rose through the ranks, becoming a gunner with the Number 2 Battery in Guelph. By 1896 he was a Lieutenant. At the University of Toronto John McCrae was a member of the Queen's Own Rifles of Canada and rose to company Captain.

In order to enlist when the South African War broke out in 1899, John asked to postpone the fellowship in pathology he had achieved at Montreal's McGill University. In South Africa, John was commissioned to lead an artillery battery from Guelph, which became part of D Battery Canadian Field Artillery. To continue with his medical career, he resigned in 1901 and returned to Canada. John McCrae was still convinced of the duty to fight for one's country, but was disillusioned and concerned about the poor care available for sick and wounded

HERE COMES THE MOON

soldiers as well as horses, on which subjects he wrote papers. In South Africa more died of illnesses than of their wounds or in battle.

By 1914 the First World War opened its jaws and it was during that war that John McCrae again volunteered for military service and took up his last medical appointments. Now 42, he was soon transferred from military to medical duties, being appointed medical officer to the First Brigade of Canadian Field Artillery with the rank of Major.

Before his departure John wrote to a friend "I am going because I think every bachelor, especially if he has experience of war, ought to go. I am really rather afraid, but more afraid to stay at home with my conscience." With him he took his horse Bonfire, given to him by John and Marjory Todd of Montreal. (John McCrae's rank entitled him to have a horse.)

It was during the Second Battle of Ypres that the Germans first unleashed their deadly new weapon: chlorine gas. In the following 17 days half the brigade died. John McCrae, surrounded by the constant cries of the dying and the sounds of guns, rifles and exploding shells wrote "The general impression in my mind is of a nightmare … and a terrible anxiety lest the line should give way." During that battle one observer said that John McCrae, who had worked virtually non-stop for 17 days, never having the time to change his clothes, aged 20 years.

In June of 1915, soon after he wrote "In Flanders Fields" John McCrae was transferred to No. 3 McGill Canadian General Hospital in France as Chief of Medical Services. His previous friends there hardly recognised him in the exhausted man who had lost his optimistic smile and nature. One said, "It was as if an icon had been broken."

Housing at No.3 McGill consisted of huge tents where the cold was bitter. They moved to the site of the ruins of the Jesuit College of Boulogne. It was here that the dog Bonneau, which belonged to the Debackers a French family living by No.3 McGill, came every day to stay with John McCrae. It was here also that he began to spend time alone on long rides with Bonfire, and seemed to have lost his enthusiasm for life and belief in the future.

Until his death on January, 28, 1918, John McCrae tended many wounded and gassed soldiers each day, experiencing the full force of the suffering of the soldiers from the most terrible battles of the First World War: Ypres, the Somme, Vimy Ridge, Arras and Passchendaele.

However, he never forgot his little nieces and nephews; John McCrae sent them letters from Bonfire signed with a hoof print. Of

MAKING A DIFFERENCE

the fame of "In Flanders Fields", John made the wry comment that never had his name been misspelled so often.

To feel even more part of the soldiers' suffering, John McCrae insisted on living in his own tent next to theirs. However, he was ordered to a warmer shelter when his health was affected by the winter cold. During the summer of 1917 John suffered severe asthma attacks and bronchitis. The day he became too ill to work, January, 24, 1918, John McCrae learned he had been appointed consulting physician to the First British Army. He was the first Canadian to be honoured in this way. His condition deteriorated into pneumonia and he was moved to the No.14 British General Hospital for Officers where on January, 28, John died of pneumonia and complications from meningitis.

Lieutenant Colonel McCrae was buried with full military honours. Bonfire was in attendance carrying his master's riding boots turned backwards. The funeral, attended by many soldiers and also the most important military people such as Sir Arthur Currie, head of the Canadian forces in Europe, was filmed and is available on the internet and also is part of the National Film Board's documentary film: *John McCrae's War – In Flanders Fields.*

In 1918, the American John Philip Sousa composed music to accompany "In Flanders Fields" (available on YouTube). Canadian school authorities have named several schools after John McCrae and in 1968 he achieved further recognition with a stamp bearing his image. Other posthumous honours followed: his being named a person of National Historic importance and also John McCrae's induction (April 23, 2015) to the Canadian Medical Hall of Fame. The induction was for his medical research which advanced our under-standing of tuberculosis, scarlet fever, nephritis and lobar pneumonia. There is a permanent memorial to John McCrae in the form of his birthplace, McCrae House in Guelph, which houses displays about his life. Two identical statues of him, created by sculptor Ruth Abernethy and entirely funded by private donations, were erected in Ottawa on May, 3, 2015 and in front of the Guelph Civic Museum June, 25, 2015.

John McCrae, poet, artist, soldier, doctor, and in all his dealings a fine human being, deserves to be honoured. We remember him.

DAILY LIFE

Spring, That Joyful Season

It was spring, my favourite time of year. The weekly emails to Josie, a childhood friend living in the UK, were full of it. She had told me she liked to hear about events in our garden. As usual I described birds dashing around trailing straw for their nests, which they lined with mud mixed with water from the creek. Then there were the drifts of forget-me-nots in the wooded part at the back, and violets all over the grass, shiny cushions of periwinkle round the trees – and then of course the truly spectacular yellow drifts of – wouldn't you know it? – dandelions.

That year we had some distinguished and unusual visitors: a pair of wood ducks. First, the female sailed majestically down in front of our house. She had pretty light-brown speckled feathers, and soon the male, in all his glorious colours, arrived. Having seen wood ducks only at a distance, swimming on a river, it was difficult for me to understand how big they were. They seemed almost as big as Canada geese. They wandered around for a short while, even perching on the branch of a tree (another unusual ability of wood ducks) and then decided against us as hosts for their nest.

For more than ten years, Josie had suffered a fatal form of bone marrow cancer – but she always bounced back after the latest treatment. Josie enjoyed my accounts of young cottontail rabbits with fluffy red fur and almost transparent ears. They come out from the middle of a clump of trees by our house for their first look at the world. Their elders have a wonderful time taking their fill of all the new good stuff that passes for grass at our place. After the first taste, before continuing with the feast, they jump for sheer joy.

That spring we saw two baby groundhogs, also with fluffy red fur, on their hind legs, front paws holding the edges of two flowerpots by our door, munching away at the leaves. It took Ronald a few comments of "Shoo" and some waving of hands before they reluctantly ambled away. All this information went into my latest news for Josie.

HERE COMES THE MOON

That morning she had replied with a question about whether we had yet seen the adult groundhog. (For years, a succession of these has lived in a hole in the roots of a maple tree opposite the kitchen window.) I was just about to answer with the news that our newest occupier of the maple tree burrow liked to wander around sniffing the spring flowers, ending up with a sunbathe on the front deck, when a new message came in. It was the monthly update on Josie for our network of childhood friends and began "I have some sad news …". That afternoon (we are five hours behind the UK) Josie, by now in long-term care, had gone down for her afternoon nap and had not wakened when called. I like to think of Josie falling asleep with visions of our garden, its flowers and wildlife in her thoughts.

She left us in spring, that most joyful of seasons. It is still my favourite time of year. I know Josie would not want it any other way.

Books

In April we had an ice storm. For four days the electricity was off, and so was our sump pump, causing a flooded basement. We hauled two heavy rugs upstairs. We also took up the bottom two rows all along the fourteen or so bookcases holding about 2,000 books from the approximately 6,000 we have accumulated. Of course the first reaction was, "We have to get rid of some of our books." The next reaction was, "Which ones?" And then came the final answer, "None."

Our books are more than just printed paper we've glanced through in the past. I look at a section of Barbara Pym novels and think of Helen, the long-time friend who first recommended that author to me. I see Lawrence Durrell's Alexandria Quartet (four books set in Alexandria, North Africa, all in the same time frame) and I remember the time I spent reading them while waiting for the birth of our first child. I recently tried re-reading one of the Alexandria Quartet books and found it didn't appeal any more. But can I bear to throw them away? I think you know the answer.

One book I spared from my clear-out of books from a later-life re-entry into academia was on Statistics. Inscribed on the fly leaf were the words "Dog food, butter, sugar," a poignant reminder of the late-night slogging after children were in bed and of the household shopping on the way from classes as I hurried to be home before the end of school. And there are the duplicates of books that my husband and I have, from our times in the same classes at university, both books carefully kept – so far.

The shelf of children's books is a particular joy. They remind me of my children's childhoods and also of episodes in my own. The Joyce Lankester series about the little girl Milly-Molly-Mandy in her English village, with the careful drawings of people and her friends and of village maps, bring back the comfort I derived from them. When I first read these books, I had been sent away from home to friends for

HERE COMES THE MOON

a few days while my father was due to be arrested by the Japanese secret police. In different circumstances, they have given great joy to my children and grandchildren.

I have always enjoyed the carefree innocence of children's books and still turn to them. Our several editions of Kenneth Grahame's *The Wind in the Willows* (a book for both adults and children) remind me of a time when one child was at kindergarten, one was having a nap, and the other was wide awake in the afternoon. So there was no nap for me. Instead, we sat up in bed, propped by pillows, and had a delightful time reading about the adventures of Ratty, Mole, Badger and Toad.

The stories by James Herriot, the veterinarian, made into the television series *All Things Bright and Beautiful* are reminders of happy holidays in Yorkshire with my English relatives. The whodunits remind me of returning to the working world when most of what I read then was murder mysteries. The collections of essays by Gregory Clark, much-loved war correspondent and newspaper columnist, remind me of our early days in Canada when we rented part of a house near his. From the sunroom where Gregory worked, he used to wave out at Katherine and me as we went to and from the park. Gregory said Katherine was the only child he'd seen who always looked back the way she had come over the side of the stroller, instead of forward.

Throw away memories of all these special people and times of our lives? Never.

The National Historic Site that Almost Never Was

During the past winter months, McCrae House in Guelph has been closed and under renovation in preparation for the Hundredth Anniversary of the world famous poem "In Flanders Fields". During the 1915 battle of Ypres, Lieutenant Colonel John McCrae wrote the poem in memory of his friends Lieutenant Alexis Helmer, who was hit by a shell and died in the battle aged 22, and Lieutenant Owen Hague.

Built in 1858, McCrae House is a typical mid-nineteenth century limestone cottage with a trellised verandah featuring climbing flowering vines, and roofed in cedar shingles. The McCrae family lived there from 1870 to 1873. In 1872, John McCrae was born in the house.

By 1966, the current owners the Aldom family had to move to another town, and put up the limestone cottage for sale. Three Legion members, who were also members of the Guelph Historical Society, put up their own houses as collateral to buy the building. With others they formed the Lieutenant Colonel John McCrae Birthplace Society.

The group's purpose was to establish a museum to honour the memory of John McCrae. In 1983, the society transferred ownership of McCrae House to the City of Guelph and it became part of Guelph Civic Museums. This made it permanently available to the whole of Canada and indeed the world: "In Flanders Fields" has aroused the interest of people globally. Because of the foresight of a small group of people, by now the site has been visited by people from countries as far apart as Australia, the United Kingdom and Japan.

In honour of the flower featured in John McCrae's poem, the entrance to McCrae House will now feature a striking poppy theme. Why the poppy? Blood red corn poppies grew across Western Europe in conditions where the earth had been unusually badly disturbed during wars such as the Napoleonic wars of the early nineteenth century. During the First World War, in northern France where the earth had been ripped apart again and again, the poppy was one of the

HERE COMES THE MOON

only plants hardy enough to grow on the battlefields. The poppy has now become the symbol of those who died in both World Wars and the following Korean War and Afghanistan conflict.

However, it was not always so. After the end of the First World War an American, Moina Belle Michael, who had worked in Europe during the war, was overwhelmed by the impact on her of "In Flanders Fields" and had the idea of adopting the flower as a symbol of the loss of life during the war. Sales of artificial poppies could also be a fundraiser to aid the many disabled and destitute veterans. Initially this went no further than the eastern United States. However in 1920 Ms. Michael, a professor at the University of Georgia and enthusiastic supporter of the YWCA, attended a YWCA conference in Europe. There, Madame Anne E. Guerin took up the idea and in 1920 travelled through France, Australia, New Zealand, Canada and the UK giving talks advocating adoption of the poppy as a symbol and fundraiser to benefit veterans. In 1921 the British Legion launched the first Poppy Day appeal, and was followed in 1922 by other Commonwealth countries, France and the United States.

Passing through into McCrae House, visitors will see new graphics, videos and timelines highlighting John McCrae's life as a soldier, adventurer, doctor, artist and poet. This month (April, 2015) his significant contributions to the field of medicine will be recognized by John McCrae's acceptance to the Medical Hall of Fame. He was nominated by the staff of Guelph Civic Museums and the Royal College of Physicians and Surgeons of Canada. At McCrae House, there are also exhibits depicting John McCrae's early life in Guelph. A major part of the display will be a presentation of "In Flanders Fields" in large-scale script on floor to ceiling panels. To show the global nature of its impact to this day, an audio presentation will indicate the many different languages into which the poem has been translated.

The award winning gardens, open to the public, and cared for by volunteers, feature plants popular in the mid-to-late nineteenth century.

The McCrae House at 108 Water Street, Guelph, Ontario N1G 1A6, is owned and operated by the City of Guelph and Guelph Civic Museums which can be contacted via the website: www.guelph.ca/museum and (519) 836-1482. This important national historic site is well worth a visit.

Elora Writers' Festival

Over the years, I have attended writers' festivals, most of them showcasing a large number of authors at booths where the literary minded can visit. There are so many admittedly good writers that the tendency is for people to sample each one for a few minutes and then move on. Some even bring folding stools or shooting sticks for a brief rest during their trek.

Sixteen years ago, I saw an advertisement for the Elora Writers' Festival, offering six writers, to be introduced three before and three after an interval for light refreshments, conversation and buying books. Those attending were expected to listen to all six. I liked this idea, but asked myself, "Is six too few?" Like Goldilocks, I found the Elora Writers' Festival to be not too big, not too small, but just the right size, and have had the opportunity to develop some good friendships among others attending.

The annual festival, which is usually sold out, has been held since 1994, the excellent writers present themselves well in a relaxed setting that has to be one of the prettiest possible.

The 2013 festival organizers changed the previous approach of an evening dinner with authors, to a party after the festival, with finger food and wine included in the ticket price. There, attendees could mingle with each other and the writers, and ask questions at a Q and A period. The gathering was a smash-hit ending to the festival, and will be repeated. A prime mover has been Roxanne Beale, owner of a successful Fergus book, cards and gifts store from which she runs other activities for local residents. Roxanne was a lively presenter, giving a friendly welcome to those at the subsequent social event.

The 2013 writers came from a variety of backgrounds from gardening, comedy and mystery to animal concerns. A most welcome aspect was the inclusion of two local writers: Carrie Snyder of Waterloo, and

HERE COMES THE MOON

Ailsa Kay who helped start the festival and has returned to live in Fergus. I bought both of their books.

After a career oriented to short fiction appearing in leading journals such as *The New Quarterly,* Ailsa Kay has written a first novel, *Under Budapest.* It is an intricately plotted, riveting tale set in the extensive underground tunnels and criminal world of Budapest before and after the lifting of the Iron Curtain. Carrie Snyder has written two books so far and will soon bring out a third. For company, she has four children 12 and under, a dog and husband. I am so impressed by Carrie Snyder's exceptional talent, that I have written reviews of her books, which follow:

Hair Hat by Carrie Snyder

I finally found a copy of this wonderful book in the University of Toronto's Robarts library. Sadly the publisher has allowed it to go out of print.

People don't have to read very far into this gem, with its eerie recurring image of the hair hat, to realize they are witnessing the debut of a major new talent. The minutely observed scenes and stories, some of which overlap, reveal an author who deeply understands the central emotions of her characters' lives.

Provided she keeps her own steady focus and is not distracted by trends or a short-term desire to please, Carrie Snyder will very likely be our next generation's Alice Munro.

The Juliet Stories by Carrie Snyder

Only two or three sentences into this remarkable novel, and the reader knows this writer has produced a piece that is easily as good as her first. Carrie Snyder is developing in a marvellous way.

In Book One, Juliet tells the story of her sojourn in Nicaragua, where her Canadian/American parents were protesting the involvement of the United States in that country's internal affairs. The child's voice and perspective of Juliet who is "almost eleven" comes through clearly in the perceptive detail that is typical of this writer. While relating the family's poignant story, Carries Snyder does a wonderful job of

DAILY LIFE

communicating to readers a picture of the heat, dust, dirt and poverty of capital city Managua. She also clearly conveys the endless destruction, tragedy and futility of war.

In Book Two, the story continues mainly in Canada and in a more episodic way, as Juliet grapples with the illness and death from cancer of her brother Keith and also with her own march to maturity. Like all those who have had an unusual childhood, Juliet carries at the back of her mind the memory of Nicaragua, something she cannot explain to others who have lived all their lives in one place.

One of the many revolving acquaintances in Nicaragua is Heinrich, whose wife is there with the Red Cross. It is masterly, the way in which Carrie Snyder slips the reader forward through time to infer the shocking manner of Heinrich's death several pages before it actually comes up in the story.

Equal to or even surpassing the plot is the writing. Just look at the second sentence in the following quotation from page five where their initial host Renate is talking through her bedroom window to Juliet's mother, Gloria, below: 'There is a park down the street.' Renate drops each word down onto Gloria's head." Such extraordinary sentences are abundant in this book. For the writing alone, *The Juliet Stories* should be slowly savoured, the sentences rolled around on the tongue.

Please come to this wonderful festival. You are sure to enjoy it and meet interesting people.

Let's Tanka

No. that's not a typo for tango; it really is an invitation to tanka. Most people have heard of the haiku, a form of Japanese poetry, but not many have encountered its precursor, the tanka. You are about to be among those fortunate few.

This form of poetic expression consists of five lines, of not more than 5,7,5,7,7 syllables each, in that sequence. If there is a group of two or more poems, a title is appropriate. As I do not translate Japanese – and a translation wouldn't work anyway – I've made up a few as illustrations (below).

Try composing your own tanka; it's fun, something like a crossword puzzle you assemble yourself. If you have a thought about something, try to express it as a poem using this format. It's an absorbing way to spend a long winter's evening, and you will have something to show for your effort at the end of the day. Tanka makes a pleasant change from that other Japanese pastime (or for some of us headache-inducing torture) the Sudoku.

Funeral

In awkward groups
They stand, reminiscing
Trying to keep Death
At bay with their stories
Of his past (there's no future)

A bird's winter call
Knifes the air. Eheu, élas …
Alas, it cries
In a timeless language
Each mourner understands.

HERE COMES THE MOON

Biological Clock

The phantom child came
This being with no body
And no name
Winding his arms
Tight around her waist.

Then, woven in air
The longed for son returned
Rested his head
On her shoulder in farewell
And slipped away forever.

He would be twenty
Now – this child she never made
And must make himself
In some shadowy dream world
Where he is strong, and handsome.

Beginnings – To an Eighteen-Year-Old

Recently, our Ink and Cookies Writing Group assigned the following homework: "What advice would you offer an eighteen-year-old who is about to graduate from high school with mediocre marks and thinks he or she would like to find employment?" Here's what I wrote:

To a young person who has worked hard and tried (as opposed to just going through the motions) but still cannot get high marks, I'd say, please understand that just because you haven't done all that well academically during the years you spent in school, you are not a failure, either now or for the rest of your life The teen years are stressful in themselves, never mind exams. Try to be an understanding friend to yourself. Many people like you go on to make a success of their lives in a broad range of fields. So first of all, "Chin up!" Not everyone can be first in class. You are still a worthwhile person, and your personality and character will be very important to your future. Not everyone can afford to attend university or is fitted for it, thank goodness, or how would we get any practical work done?

By actually graduating, you have shown you have developed the ability to work hard in adverse circumstances and not give up. You did not drop out. In that, you have shown you have character. Character and the ability to work hard and never give up are very important in making a success of your life. Believe me, high school is not the be all and end all. There is life after High School. School years are only a small fraction of your life. You have a whole new world before you, and many years of it.

An upstanding person like you are will find a job although it may not pay well. However, a year earning at minimum wage can be a good experience. During that year you should think carefully what you want to do later in your life: will that low-paying job be the bottom rung of a ladder or a dead end? Think about what further training you will need – and you probably will need some. Before you graduate, try some of

HERE COMES THE MOON

the aptitude tests available at school to use as a guide for your next move. Talk to your family and friends. They will have noticed abilities you have that you may not have noticed yourself – or even problems with the way you handle people. A round peg doesn't fit into a square hole, so try to find out where you do fit in. Now is the time to take stock. Now is the time to widen your interests, see the new horizons. And now is the time to start succeeding at what you really want to do.

If your dreams do not work out – perhaps through lack of money – you will still make a success of something. Be proud of what you do, even if it seems mundane to others, and do it well, because all work is worthwhile. Go forward calmly, and never fear as some do when they are in high school, about being alone all their lives. You will find a companion who will love and appreciate you as a person and walk beside you in that new life.

Stop, We're Canadian

Have you ever watched the news on an American television station? When the weatherman has his turn, up comes a map of North America, with the top half filled in an anonymous yellow colour. The high winds from Illinois end abruptly at the yellow part of the continent. After dumping several feet of the white stuff on Maine, snowstorms battering the east coast magically disappear. It's as if thousands of teeny tiny (given the scale of the map) border guards are standing there with their hands up saying "We don't want your nasty weather. In fact we don't want anything unpleasant at all. Stop, we're Canadian."

Even the hurried, five-minutes-for-the-whole-planet's-weather BBC World News's forecast, shows North America as a whole and highlights Vancouver, Winnipeg and Montreal. Lately, they've even been mentioning Toronto. Why is it that the American broadcasters put our part of the continent in yellow and don't even give it a general label: CANADA? Do they hate us so much? Not at all, it seems to me that they simply don't know anything about us. The American weather forecasters probably didn't "do" Canada in their school geography lessons.

Imagine a horrified American weatherman with the wrong map up on his screen: a map of the whole of North America, the weather systems continuing on their merry way north. What is he to say when that snowstorm battering the east coast continues up past Maine – to where? – passing through that large island to the northeast – called what? – before petering out, fortunately for him, in the Atlantic (a part of the known world)?

The Oxford Canadian Dictionary describes Canada as "the second largest country in the world, covering the entire northern half of N. America with the exception of Alaska." However, our population is not the second largest, being only half that of the (much smaller in area) United Kingdom, and one-tenth that of the United States. A Wikipedia

77

HERE COMES THE MOON

list puts Canada's population at 37th among the world's nations, and a puny 0.49 percent of the total. With the recent exception of the former mayor of Toronto, Rob Ford, Canada does not usually hit the world's headlines. Again, we are peaceable folk (we even keep the peace in troubled countries abroad), also mostly well behaved and, insofar as we are known internationally, known for our good manners. These are not headline-making qualities, a factor that goes a long way to explain why many, including the American weather forecasters, don't know much about us.

In the autobiographical section of my website (margaretblair.com) I say that my husband and I "have been fortunate to live most of our lives in Canada, a capable, modest and decent country with a distinctive culture to which Canadians take a restrained approach." Canada may be the world's best-kept secret. I, for one, am content to keep it exactly the way it is.

Have You Ever Wondered?

… where those little fake mice you give your cats go? We have regularly given out one mouse each to our cats, only to have them disappear (the mice not the cats). We've looked under couches, beds and other low-lying furniture only to have to hand out more mice.

Recently, we found out what happens to the little critters. Our washer and dryer broke down and we ordered new ones. When people came to remove the failed appliances, there under where they'd been were dozens of little fake mice, rather chewed. Our cats enjoyed batting them down the stairs to the laundry area, and whizzing them across the slippery linoleum on the floor, only to have the mice swallowed up under the appliances. That also explained something else: why we sometimes found disconsolate cats hanging around down there. We still hand out fake mice to our cats, and made sure the new appliances were on wheels.

As avid readers, we read practically anything, including notices posted on the side of the road when we're driving – always also trying to pay enough attention not to end up, like the American humorist Ogden Nash's John Brown, "under a slab" because he "watched the ads and not the road." A fascinating aspect of billboards is the apostrophes. Signs flash by advertising "Frie's", "Lady's Shoe's" and "Hour's Open for Business". And what about those strange announcements like "W inter ish ere" or "Stor ge un its"? These are easy to decipher, but are they put up that way deliberately? It seems not. The wind probably blows the letters around. One that really had us mystified was "BEALERT". Being attentive readers, we immediately thought of Roxanne Beale who runs Roxanne's Reflections book and gift store in Fergus. This must be an announcement of an honour or degree; perhaps Registered Something beginning with T (RT). Could it even be *Royal* something beginning with T? It was only after thinking of BEALERT before sleeping and

HERE COMES THE MOON

referring the matter to our subconscious minds to sort out overnight, that we woke up with the solution: BE ALERT.

Have you ever wondered about the use of the word "progress" as in "you can't stand in the way of progress"? And wondered why, in this context, progress always seems to involve some destruction of the environment and habitat for animals? And why, in comparison to thirty years ago, is the joyful dawn chorus of birds so muted now? Could it be due to the progress we've made?

South Sea Islands and Fire-breathing Dragons

Our post office people have commented that they have never seen so many catalogues going to one household as go to ours. I have to admit they're all for me; but let me tell you my side of the story.

I started the habit when as a stay-at-home mother of young children I found the Eaton's catalogue an absolute godsend. It contained everything I needed in household wares, clothes, cloth for making shorts and tops, all sewing necessities including a machine, and even knitting wools and needles.

I could order these by telephone, and they duly arrived, conveniently paid for at the end of the month via the Eaton's credit card, and brought to the door by the Eaton's deliveryman. He knew who we were and waved from his van to the children and me when we were out for our daily walk.

Out of sheer sentimentality, I kept the last Eaton's catalogue ever, issued in 1976. Looking at the high prices for household goods (some higher in 1976 dollars than they are in today's) relative to the incomes at that time, has proved invaluable for tracking how prosperous we have become since.

The Metropolitan Museum catalogue came annually from New York with offerings of superior Christmas cards, and each fall, Dominion Seed House catalogue joined Eaton's with a detailed and poetic description of an extraordinary variety of seeds. I once grew a trailing Japanese something-or-other on our dining room window ledge. The plant grew down three feet of thick moss green foliage dotted with tiny chrysanthemum-like flowers – until it dragged itself to death one night, leaving a mess all over the carpet.

Then came the revolution, when magazines and catalogues started to sell their subscriber lists to new start-ups. This resulted in a flood of unsolicited mail, some of it quite useful. I still scour Hampstead House Books for anything about Rupert Bear, a favourite still of my teenaged grandchildren and me.

HERE COMES THE MOON

Some catalogues are highly entertaining. Hammacher Schlemmer, among their usual high quality, useful and rather expensive wide variety of offerings, often have something unusual for sale. One winter, I was enchanted by an inflatable South Sea Island, complete with palm tree, sandy beach and a sun lamp – bliss – and was working out how to change furniture round to accommodate it in front of the fire, when I noticed the price – already inflated – and changed my mind. Right now (2015) through Hammacher Schlemmer, you can buy a nine-foot-long, remote-controlled and jet-powered fire-breathing flying dragon – for a mere $60,000 (USD).

However, a few years ago, there came the start of a slightly sinister development. One of our magazines had my name as Marguerite, and for Christmas a catalogue arrived to that name from the Smithsonian Institution, with its somewhat garish jewellery and war-oriented clothes for children, rather different from offerings from the Metropolitan Museum. More catalogues for Marguerite came by mail: jigsaw puzzles and tacky clothing, all sorts of "stuff" I wouldn't want. I threw out all of them.

Design Toscano switched their original, more classical offerings of statues and plinths to those of a totally different style. Discouraged by my refusal to purchase gargoyles, fairies and those pesky dragons, they stopped sending their catalogues to me. However, undaunted, after a few months they started sending them to my alter ego: Marguerite.

A last straw came in the form of a catalogue offering underwear so brief I could hardly see it. The vaguely pornographic nature of the illustrations offended my Scottish Presbyterian tastes and I decided this had to stop. Obviously, Marguerite had a totally different personality from my own. (Is it possible that somewhere, there is a real Marguerite Blair who is puzzling over the inappropriate catalogues she receives for Margaret?)

I love my catalogues and always read right through them; that is to say *my* catalogues, but not Marguerite's; those have to go. So far, despite sending them back with a "no more please" note, and even a follow-up phone call, I have been unable to stem the flow, some might say "avalanche" – but I will over time. Until I manage to accomplish this, no doubt to the great relief of the postal services, I've decided to keep calm by taking up meditation. It is highly regarded and useful. So let's take a deep breath in … slowly breathe out … Ahhh …

Thanksgiving

Call of wild geese flying south
Field of sunflowers
Scurry of squirrels storing food
In the pine tree boughs
Silk sprouting from corn stalk tops
Ripened by soft rain

Drawn by three gorgeous horses,
A Mennonite ploughs
Fertile brown furrows of earth
Waiting for next spring
Sunset over lake water
Tawny yellow hay

Maples' splendour of colour
Smile at the first sip of tea
Each in its own way gives thanks
For another peaceful year.

Alexander Telfer recovering from First World War wounds

Remembrance

In Flanders fields the poppies bloomed around the graves of soldiers, nature's reminder of the deaths of the very young with their lives before them. The very young, tragic cannon fodder, fighting the war of their elders, these elders securely ensconced in their clubs and offices. We have a large harvest of poems written by First World War soldiers turned poets, poignant messages to posterity about their heightened perception of nature and love of life, as they faced their deaths – and so many did die, including our own famous poet, Colonel John McCrae (MAKING A DIFFERENCE above).

Each month in legion halls there is the tender affirmation from Lawrence Binyon's poem "For the Fallen" that "They will not grow old, as we that are left grow old: age shall not weary them, nor the years condemn. At the going down of the sun and in the morning, we will remember them." with the response, "We will remember them." In the legions, these young dead are truly not forgotten, year round.

The poem concludes with these evocative lines: "To the innermost heart of their own land they are known/ … As the stars that are starry in the time of our darkness,/To the end, to the end, they remain."

On November 11 not only are the dead remembered in a large national service but also all across Canada, in each small town, in a smaller service of remembrance at 11:00 am. Below a statue of a soldier, are inscribed the names of all the local young men who died in war. The last names are often still familiar today as their descendants live on in the area.

But what happened to the weary survivors of this war to end all wars, those brave soldiers, across the world, returning with their recurring flashbacks (now, but not then, given a name: post traumatic stress disorder; now, but not then, given medical treatment and a disability pension)? What happened to their fiancées, wives, parents, sisters, dealing with the howling nightmares, their children, those others

HERE COMES THE MOON

widowed and orphaned by the war; those mutilated families, what of them? How did these valiant people manage to go on with their lives, year after year after year? This is the tale of one such group.

A snapshot of my father's family before the war shows the father, John, an engineer employed at a substantial salary. Three elder sons, Jock, Jim and Will, had a thriving accounting and bookkeeping business together. Isabella (Belle), the elder of two daughters, both engaged to be married, held a secretarial position at Collins Publishing House and her sister, Helen (Nell), helped their mother, Elizabeth, in the home. They all lived together in a large apartment on the top floor of a substantial Victorian sandstone building in what is now part of the preserved heritage in Glasgow, Scotland. My father, Alexander, the youngest son aged 15, having won a full scholarship, had started studies at the Glasgow School of Art. Also at the age of 15, he had completed his university entrance exams and at 18 would go on to Glasgow University after completion of the art studies. All was prosperous and well.

Then the First World War opened its jaws. Aunt Belle's fiancée and Jim were killed. By two years after the war's end, of the five wage earners only one, Aunt Belle, survived. Jock returned suffering from sleeping sickness. Will had severe shellshock and never again worked full time. My father, who had enlisted at a recruitment booth conveniently situated near the School of Art, needed two years of surgery on his ankle before he recovered. Soon after the war's end, their mother Elizabeth died of a heart attack suffered after attending a Victory parade, quickly followed by their father, John.

Through the long years following, the remaining family, and there were many like them across the Western world, pulled together. For obvious financial reasons, my father abandoned his pre-war plans and left for Shanghai, China, where he joined the Shanghai Municipal Council's police force becoming superintendent of the Criminal Investigation Department. Until 1941, when another war reached the Far East, he sent substantial monthly cheques to help his sisters and especially for the support of Jock, who was cared for at home until his death in 1939. It was only then that the younger aunt, Nell, married. By that time, she and her faithful Davie were too old to have children, of which there were none from that large family, except my brother and me.

Like most survivors, our father rarely mentioned the War. How could he, or any of the survivors, describe the experience: the cold,

DAILY LIFE

terror, hunger, exhaustion they felt, the lice, rats, slime, body parts with which they routinely shared their space?

But there were little snatches of information followed by silence. Usually when there was time for reflection on one of our walks in the country outside the town where we lived, my father would suddenly remember. He once told me about being buried alive in an explosion. There was a small pocket of air and my father debated whether to use it slowly to hang on to his life a little longer, or use it up quickly to call for help. My father chose the latter action and was rescued, the only survivor from his battalion. He was cared for at a military field hospital and sent back to fight. The soldiers were told not to drink water from wells which might be poisoned. My father described how his tongue swelled up from lack of fluid. On another of our walks, he described how he was seriously wounded in an explosion and he and his unarmed stretcher bearers on their way to the field hospital met a German soldier with his gun ready to fire. However, in an act of mercy, the German allowed them to pass. Later, when travelling by train for evacuation to Britain, my father was in great pain and was gritting his teeth hanging on to a divider between his bunk and that of the next wounded man. The other soldiers called and called for a nurse to come and give him pain-killers. When they arrived at the other end, a nurse asked about my father's wife and children. Still a teenager, only recently 18, he must have aged during his experiences. My father's photo, taken while he was convalescent, shows him as having recovered a younger appearance. This is how young the soldiers were, some younger, as young as 15.

Like many other fathers who survived war, our father was always a compassionate and wonderful father, never allowing the negative experiences to affect his relations with us. As well, like other families dealing with the aftermath of war, the remaining family in Scotland kept up a cheerful front. With respect and affection we remember our father and his family, and many like them across the world. We honour them for the long years they spent, without complaint, dealing with the effects of the First World War.

Statistics released a few years after the War's end showed that over 37 million soldiers were killed, wounded or missing. France suffered a particularly high death rate. One-third of France's young men of fighting age died. It took over a generation to replenish the French population – just in time for the Second World War.

Back Row from Left: Golliwog, Raggedy Andy
Front Row from Left: Rabbit, China Doll, Rupert Bear

Raggedy Ann, Golliwog and Little Black Sambo

The other day, looking at some of my children's old toys and thinking of Christmas, I began to wonder what happened to the golliwog (I don't see my grandchildren with any) and the book about Little Black Sambo beloved by my children. And what about the Raggedy Ann and Andy with embroidered faces and button eyes that mothers used to make from McCall's patterns?

The American writer Johnny Gruelle (1880-1936) created Raggedy Ann for his daughter Marcella; the first book about the doll came out in 1918, soon followed by one about Raggedy Andy in 1920. Some books about the two dolls have been in print ever since and one is even available in a Kindle edition.

Up until the 1960s, McCall's patterns for the two dolls were readily available for that era's stay-at-home mothers to make for their children. In 1980 I decided to make Raggedy Ann for a friend, whose mother had died when she was young and who had never had such a doll made for her. I discovered the patterns had been discontinued due to lack of demand. All the mothers including me had gone to work outside the home. What I could find (and I bought it and made the doll) was a leftover pattern for a giant Raggedy Ann three feet tall.

So where did homemade Raggedy Ann and Andy go? It seems they went to the mass market and catalogues, with faces mainly painted on rather than embroidered. On the Internet, I did find one original McCall's pattern "like new" for sale at a reasonable price, but decided to leave it for someone else to make for her grandchildren. Mine have inherited their parents' long-lasting dolls.

Like Raggedy Ann and Andy, Little Black Sambo came from the imagination of an author, Helen Bannerman. Born in Edinburgh in 1862, she spent most of her life in Madras, India, with her medical officer husband. Little Black Sambo may look African, but he is really Indian. He speaks of the tigers that had stolen his beautiful new clothes

89

HERE COMES THE MOON

as quarrelling with each other and turning into *ghee*, the Indian melted butter, which Sambo's mother, Black Mumbo, used to make delicious pancakes for the family, including father, Black Jumbo.

Black Sambo has gone the way of political correctness, reappearing in 1965 as the much less popular White Squibba. She was written about in notes by Helen Bannerman and made into a book, *Little White Squibba*, completed from these notes by her daughter, Day. An interesting aside is that Bannerman's grandson Tom Kibble was part of the University of Edinburgh's Physics team who discovered the Higgs-Kibble mechanism and from there the famous Higgs boson (explanation of that another time and not from me).

Like the Raggedy toys, Golliwog first came to light in a book, *The Adventures of Two Dutch Dolls and a Golliwogg* published in 1895, by the British author and illustrator Florence Kate Upton. The golliwog figure featured in other children's books, notably the Noddy ones by Enid Blyton. The distinguished art historian Sir Kenneth Clark said the golliwogs of his childhood "were examples of chivalry far more persuasive than the unconvincing knights of Arthurian legend."

In the 1890s, the cakewalk took over in popularity as a dance in America. Originally a parody by slaves of their upper-class white masters' dancing, it was the first black dance to cross over to American whites. Many upper-class white summer resorts featured a Cakewalk as the finale to the season. It inspired the composer Debussy to create "The Golliwog's Cakewalk" in 1913 as part of a suite for his daughter then aged three.

Robertson's jams adopted the image as their mascot and exchanged golliwog pins for proof of purchase of their products. Children across the English-speaking world embraced the golliwog toy, and until the 1980s only the teddy bear surpassed it in popularity. But then it seems to have gone away. Why?

Golliwog all but disappeared in a storm of political correctness and defence of their image by blacks and sympathetic whites. In the 1980s Enid Blyton's Golly was replaced by the white Mr. Sparks, and by 2002 Robertson's retired the image saying it was no longer popular. In Scotland, one African-British mother had the golliwog depicted on an old mural in her child's daycare centre painted over. In Britain anyway, politicians lost their jobs if they dared defend the golliwog as a harmless children's toy. In 2011, two of them used the golliwog in a campaign against political correctness and were duly expelled from

90

DAILY LIFE

their party. However, at least in the United Kingdom, the view that the toy is offensive appears to have won. In 2007, Greater Manchester Police confiscated two golliwogs from a shop after complaints.

Recently, a shop in the Queen's estate was found to be selling golliwogs and they were quietly removed from the shelves. However, more arrived in another British store and according to the owner were "sold out in no time." In Canada, where the toy is legal, the response has been quieter as usual, and in Japan golliwogs are still as popular as they ever were before in the English-speaking world.

What are we to make of all this? I suppose if they upset some people so much we shouldn't have these books or toys. But surely small children know no bounds of race. Our son has grown up to be respectful of and friends with people of other races than our own. Yet I can't help remembering him as an almost three-year-old and his instant love at first sight for a golliwog. He spent all his money for Christmas presents on it, much to the annoyance of an older sister: I hadn't explained to him that the Christmas present money was to buy presents for other people – not for himself.

Christmas Reading

As we complete the final hustle and bustle of Christmas preparations, there comes a day when the dark fruit cake has had its final brushing of brandy, baking done in advance is in the freezer, other food is bought and presents wrapped. On the coffee table are the usual several holiday issues of magazines from years ago with their sermons from clerics and special holiday essays from prominent authors to browse through, "The Night Before Christmas" illustrated by Tasha Tudor and pop-up Christmas ABCs. A jigsaw of a Christmas scene is also there to add to as we go by.

Then, usually after the flurry of the event itself, we relax. In the house is the still fresh scent of spruce brought in from the snowy garden to decorate the mantelpiece and tops of picture frames; another log goes on the fire, we stretch ourselves out on a couch … and read. I have a few favourite books I enjoy re-reading, such as *Wind in the Willows*, Anthony Trollope's Barchester novels and *The Tao of Pooh* by Benjamin Hoff, but each year I look for something new, something pleasant, cozy and cheerful with a happy ending to take me to the time when I turn in for the night.

This year I eagerly opened the special December book review issue of my favourite newspaper, *The New York Times* (favourite because the writers go straight to the point producing short, well-written and informative commentary on the world around us) – only to be disappointed. The first fiction choices started "With great sadness and much hard truth … etc" and "This emotionally wrenching novel … etc." or " … a feverish novel (about) … a tortured embezzler on the run." The children's section was full of improving stories about relationships and also didactic stories, one about Roget and his thesaurus. There was little that was what I knew I or my grandchildren would enjoy, sitting with our feet up beside a crackling fire. I wondered whatever happened to the relaxed, entertaining book about ordinary people with

HERE COMES THE MOON

some problems along the way and a happy ending, and decided to make up my own, short list.

The reader can't go wrong with one of the Lillian Jackson Braun "Cat Who ..." detective series, described as " ... as comforting as a warm cat on your lap on a rainy day," or "Read these books if you want to forget your troubles." A similarly calm series with good writing and plotting is the one by Ellis Peters set in medieval England and featuring Cadfael of Shrewsbury Abbey. Both these writers are deceased. However, Nancy Atherton is very much alive, and my favourites from her cozy mystery Aunt Dimity series set in England are the first one, *Aunt Dimity's Death* and a later one, *Aunt Dimity's Christmas*. Alexander McCall Smith is still active and the phenomenal success of his stories is an indication of readers' desire for something pleasant, amusing and well written. Alexander McCall Smith's 44 Scotland Street is at once poignant and hilarious. He weaves in a subtle sub-text from his background in ethics. For children I can recommend any Rupert Bear annual (there's a new one each year). The bright colours and happy varied stories with puzzles are bound to amuse and cheer a child. (I can't resist taking a look myself. For adults, there's a Followers of Rupert club to join.) And of course there's *Little Black Sambo*, a perennial favourite still in print, and the Harry Potter series, though it's not very relaxing.

Or why not unwind to a DVD of *The Wind in the Willows* (the Mark Hall and Brian Cosgrove version) or the BBC's Miss Marple series with Joan Hickson, the ultimate Miss Marple, in the role, or another favourite feel good DVD, *Enchanted April*?

It seems a pity the new children's offerings are so biased towards informing and improving our young people. What are we to do about this insistence by the publishers on putting out so many books about important social problems and illnesses, not to mention explicit sex and violence? Perhaps I'll start a petition on the internet, for more of the cozy kind of books.

A Poem for the Season

This piece, titled "Christmas Cozy," is written in four verses, each of five lines, using the format of tanka, a forerunner of the better-known haiku.

Christmas Cozy

Cat curled asleep
Tea with mince pies
Crackling wood fire
Bright polished brass
Shining in candlelight.

Visit with family
Grandchildren warmly wrapped
Building snowman with
Carrot nose, pipe and muffler
Sliding down snowy hillsides

Baking and knitting
Carollers on Christmas Eve
Frosty walks to the post box
Bright, cleaned windows to look through
At pine trees dusted with snow.

Chocolates from Belgium
Not too many
Dark brandied fruitcake
Not too much
Christmas munch

Carols on the Sixth Line

A tradition of more than 30 years, is carol singing on Christmas Eve outside the houses along the east part of the Sixth Line where we live. Over the years, the composition of the carolling group has changed, as has the population of our "street" itself. Now, we have a part of the group from Mennonite families who have kindly learned our carols, which are different from their own.

We know the singers are here from the slamming of car doors and the laughter of the children who, wrapped up well against the cold, come to sing with their parents and often grandparents. One year the road had been ploughed but not the laneway leading from it to our house. We settled in for an evening of reading and resigned ourselves to eating by ourselves the shortbread cookies we usually give out to the carollers. However, there was a sudden knock at the door and the laughter of children, and outside were the singers. They had parked cars on the road and walked up our path, well protected from the snow in sturdy wellington boots.

The concert always starts with a request from the household. One year, having found on several Christmas Eves that my favourite "The Holly and the Ivy" was not well known to the carollers, I decided to change my request. When I said, "Hark the Herald Angels Sing" there was a shout of laughter: they had just spent half an hour practising "The Holly and the Ivy."

After a few carols, the singing ends with "We Wish You a Merry Christmas." Everyone turns toward the cars, children are counted to see no one's left behind, and off the carol singers go to the next house along the Line. We go back in, make another cup of tea and settle down to our reading feeling that Christmas has truly arrived.

The Author

Margaret Blair MA, MBA, has enjoyed three careers: as a teacher, social and financial marketing researcher, mother of three and grandmother of three.

She is the author of two books on Shanghai of the 1930s and 1940s: one a memoir (*Gudao, Lone Islet, The War Years in Shanghai*) and one a historical novel (*Shanghai Scarlet*). Margaret is also the author of *Toronto's Last Rainbow* set in 1969 to 1970 Toronto. She lives with her husband, a professor emeritus of the University of Toronto, beside a stream, among Mennonite farms in southwest Ontario, Canada.

For more: www.margaretblair.com

Suggested Discussion Guide for Book Clubs

- Discuss your overall view of *Here Comes the Moon*.

- What, if anything, do you like about this book?

- What, if anything, do you dislike about this book?

- Did the beginning spark your interest?

- Which section did you enjoy the most?

- Did you learn anything from the book that you did not know before?

- In what ways do you perceive life in rural Ontario and in cities like Toronto or smaller ones like Guelph as being different from each other?

CPSIA information can be obtained
at www.ICGtesting.com
Printed in the USA
LVOW07s0506120118
562773LV00001BA/19/P